CONTENTS

D0469363

ABOUT THE AUTHOR

Gwen Bailey has always owned dogs and worked at a local kennels throughout her childhood. She has a B.Sc. (Hons) in Zoology and pioneered the use of dog behaviour knowledge in the rehoming of unwanted animals. She was Head of Animal Behaviour for one of Britain's leading charities for 12 years where she successfully solved behaviour problems in thousands of rehomed dogs, helping to prevent dogs with behavioural problems being passed from home to home and improving their rehoming success rate.

She also introduced concepts such as puppy socialization and assessment of dogs in kennels to working practices to improve welfare and increase efficiency of rehoming, and trained a team of behavourists to improve the quality of rehoming work at all of the charity's centres. Since then, she has helped many rescues around the world to gain the knowledge necessary to improve their practices.

In June 2002, she founded Puppy School (see page 189) which aims to set up a UK network of puppy class tutors who will provide good-quality puppy training and education at classes within easy reach of all owners throughout the UK. Tutors are carefully selected and trained in reward-based training methods and animal behaviour so that they can offer socialization and training classes run to a very high standard. In its first year, the network of tutors helped train over 1,500 puppies and hopes to provide education and advice to many more in the future.

Gwen has written eight books on the subject of the training, education and behaviour of dogs and cats, and many information leaflets. She is a member of the Association of Pet Behaviour Counsellors.

INTRODUCTION

For many years I have been involved in trying to mend broken relationships between dogs and their owners and changing dogs' problem behaviour to prevent them from being given up to rescue centres. This has allowed me to study man's best friend and our relationship with him in great detail which has been an amazing and fascinating experience.

Over the years it has struck me just how many people have difficulties of one sort of another, sometimes at specific points in the dog's development and sometimes continuously throughout the dog's life. As I learned more, I realized how easy it is to put those small problems right. Changing the way the owner deals with their dog can bring real improvements in their pet's behaviour and result in them having the dog they always wanted. There are benefits for the dog too since it is no longer at odds with its owners over various issues and life runs more smoothly.

Getting owners to change their ways can be difficult, particularly if they have spent a lifetime treating dogs in certain ways. They will only do so if they can see how life seems from their dog's perspective and how their actions have a direct consequence for their pet.

By increasing the owner's understanding of how dogs think and view the world, a considerable improvement can be made in the dog's welfare and well being.

Through this book, I hope that owners can reach a better understanding of their dogs and build better, stronger relationships with their pets. The advantages for the owner are an improvement in their dog's willingness to please, a faster and better response to commands and a general all-round improvement in behaviour. For the dog, the advantages are even greater since its owner will suddenly become the owner it always wanted: an owner who understands it, treats it in a way that is neither aggressive or unexplainable, and who protects it and provides for all its essential needs.

In this world, few dogs can boast of such an owner and it is my hope that there will be many more contented owners and well behaved dogs in the future.

CHOOSING A DOG

Raising a dog is fun and can be one of life's most rewarding experiences. Time and care taken during the first year to educate your puppy into an ideal adult will be well rewarded. However, the information you need is often lacking when you acquire your dog.

Almost every owner would like a dog that is loyal, well behaved, friendly, and obeys every command, but most people live with a dog whose behaviour is less than perfect and they are tolerant of a wide variety of behaviours that do not conform to their idea of good conduct. However, it is possible for everyone to have a well-behaved dog. All you need do is to develop a better understanding of your dog and to change your behaviour towards him. This book will help you to do this.

Left: Taking on an adult dog that you have saved from an uncertain future can be a very rewarding experience.

A NEW PUPPY

Before beginning the education of a young puppy, a careful choice of the raw material is essential. Choosing a puppy with the right genetic make-up is not difficult and will help to avoid disappointment as your puppy grows into an adult. Not only will it make the job of raising your puppy easier but it will also increase the likelihood that you end up with a dog that is right for you and your family. Carefully selecting not only the breed but also the strain or line from which your puppy comes will help to ensure success. A dog's adult character depends on both the genes passed on to him by his parents and ancestors and the environment he has lived in throughout his life. Both will affect his personality, temperament and qualities, and, consequently, the way in which he behaves.

Right: It is easy to fall in love with a puppy so think carefully about which breed of dog would suit you before you begin to visit breeders.

Genetic influences

Genes influence both character and behaviour. Dogs are descendants of wolves: efficient predators of large prey that hunt cooperatively in packs. Successful wolves are sociable and communicate well, traits that make them excellent precursors of domestic dogs.

Wolves have an instinctive hunting behaviour which gave them a suitable template to exploit in order to produce breeds of different abilities. We selected the

Above: Terriers enjoy games with toys that squeak because they were bred to catch and kill small animals.

qualities we most admired and created a range of dogs for different purposes. For example, collies are born with a strong instinct to chase and herd moving objects; and terriers enjoy shake and kill games, especially with objects that squeak.

The environment

While genes have given our dogs their blueprint for behaviour, the environment in which they live helps develop and strengthen behaviour patterns. Dogs that are raised and kept in different situations will have different characters. A pet dog raised from an early age in a kind home with children and animals is likely to be friendly and sociable, whereas a dog kept shut away for most of the time is likely to be shy and fearful.

Right: Good early experiences will result in a relaxed, friendly adult dog.

Early experiences

Experiences early in life, particularly during the first year, will have the most influence on a dog's future character. However, dogs are very adaptable and will continue to change their behaviour as a result of their experiences and influences from their surroundings throughout their lives. It is impossible to say whether genes or environmental factors have more influence on a dog's adult character. Both play their part and are inextricably linked.

Breed characteristics

Different breeds of dog have different characteristics and some breeds are more popular than others. Over the page you will find some useful guidelines on choosing which breed is right for you. However, this is meant only to be a basic guide and is based on experiences of the overall characteristics of the different breeds and the people who usually own them successfully. There will always be exceptions.

Mongrels and crossbreds

When considering which dog to choose, it is important not to forget the mongrel (a mixture of a number of breeds), or crossbred (usually the first cross from two pure-bred dogs). These dogs have an intrinsic value of their own and their individuality makes each of them unique. They are renowned for having a more healthy constitution than pedigree dogs which are more susceptible to inherited health problems due to their being bred from a smaller number of individuals.

MONGRELS

These contain elements of their various 'pure bred' parents. They will have a real mixture of genetic traits which can be accentuated or played down by their owners as they are raised. They are good 'all-round' dogs and often make excellent pets.

CROSSBREDS

These contain a mixture of characteristics of both breeds. The most successful crosses are often those where a breed with a gentle, placid nature is crossed with a breed with a more reactive temperament.

Right: Every mongrel is totally unique. Their genes will offer a variety of traits and they are less prone to inherited diseases.

WHICH BREED IS RIGHT FOR YOU?

By making a careful choice of a puppy or an adult dog, you will ensure that you acquire a dog with a genetic make-up that suits you. Here are some of the most popular breeds for you to consider.

German Shepherd Dog

- Bred for herding and guarding
- Activity level: high
- Characteristics: alert, attentive, tireless

Labrador Retriever

- Bred for retrieving fish and game from icy water
- Activity level: medium
- Characteristics: good-tempered, very agile, biddable

Border Collie/ working sheepdog

- Bred for herding sheep
- Activity level: high
- Characteristics: persistent, hard-working, compliant

West Highland White Terrier

- Bred for killing rats and foxes
- Activity level: high
- Characteristics: active, resolute, high self-esteem

Jack Russell Terrier

- Bred for killing rats and foxes
- Activity level: high
- Characteristics: alert, courageous, tenacious

English Springer Spaniel

- Bred for flushing and retrieving game
- Activity level: high
- Characteristics: friendly, biddable, energetic

Golden Retriever

- Bred for retrieving game
- Activity level: low
- Characteristics: alert, attentive, tireless

Cocker Spaniel

- Bred for flushing and retrieving game
- Activity level: high
- Characteristics: bustling, exuberant, affectionate

Staffordshire Bull Terrier

- Bred for fighting other dogs
- Activity level: medium
- Characteristics: fearless, courageous, tenacious

Yorkshire Terrier

- Bred for killing rats
- Activity level: medium
- Characteristics: alert, intelligent, spirited

Cavalier King Charles Spaniel

- Bred for companionship
- Activity level: low
- Characteristics: affectionate, friendly

Boxer

- Bred for hunting bears and boars
- Activity level: high
- Characteristics: lively, strong, loyal

THE RIGHT DOG FOR YOU

When looking at the characteristics for each breed, you should realize there is a negative side to each quality if it is incorrectly channelled. Although it may be beneficial to have an 'alert' dog that responds to all your requests quickly, a dog that is responsive to every little noise would become very tiresome. Similarly, a 'lively' and 'energetic' dog is great if you have a high activity level but when you have no desire to be active, this energy may emerge in unwanted activity and bad behaviour. Choosing the characteristics that suit you is essential to achieving a happy partnership.

Temperament and lifestyle

When attempting to choose the right type of dog for your character and situation, you should consider the temperament of the people in your family and also the kind of lifestyle you will want your dog to lead. This makes it more likely that you will end up with a dog that you will enjoy and that will be right for you.

YOUR PERSONALITY

Finding a dog that will be just right for you depends on your own personality type and that of other family members. Are you gentle with animals or do you take a 'no-nonsense' approach? Do you always give in to demands or do you like to get your own way?

Matching your character to that of your dog can save a lot of problems later. Are you fun-loving or sedate? Do you want a close bond with your dog or would you prefer to be more independent? Are you loud and boisterous, or quiet and gentle? Thinking about your personality will help you choose a puppy that will grow into an adult that suits you.

YOUR LIFESTYLE

You should also consider your dog's likely lifestyle as an adult. Are you a sociable family which needs a dog to be good with visitors, or do you prefer your dog to be suspicious of strangers? Do you like to go on long, energetic walks, or are you a family of couch-potatoes? Will your dog be taken everywhere with you, or will it be left at home for long periods?

Right: Are you fun-loving or are you more sedate? Springer Spaniels usually fit in well with happy, fun-loving families.

EDUCATING A PUPPY

If you choose a puppy rather than an adult dog, you start with a relatively clean slate. Raising a puppy takes a lot of time and effort but at least the mistakes, or lack of them, will be all yours.

Socializing your puppy

Most ways of achieving good dog behaviour are common to both adult dogs and puppies but a most important area that relates specifically to puppies is socialization. One of the primary requirements of a

Above: Having plenty of happy times with children and adults helps a puppy grow up into a friendly adult.

Below: Socialization with adults and children should begin early and continue throughout your puppy's development. It is one of the most essential processes for a pet dog.

pet dog is that he is friendly with people and other animals. This will depend on the quantity and quality of social contact he gets with them as he grows up.

WITH PEOPLE

The early weeks of a puppy's life are very important. During the first 12 weeks, he will approach anything unfamiliar without caution. Meeting plenty of people, including children, makes it more likely he will be unafraid and sociable in later life. If kept only with dogs for the first six months of their life, puppies will reserve their social behaviour for other dogs and will act like wild animals when faced with humans.

Therefore it is essential that socialization with people is carried out well and thoroughly while a puppy is still very young if it is to grow into a successful and well behaved pet dog.

WITH ANIMALS

A puppy also needs to be socialized with its own kind so that it remains friendly and interactive with the other dogs it meets. In addition, it should be socialized with other animals that we keep as pets, such as cats, rabbits, hamsters and small birds.

Above: Socialization also needs to take place with other animals that your puppy may encounter in later life.

Right: Teaching puppies how to greet visitors is essential and will be easier if they have been properly socialized with humans early in their lives.

WITH EVERYDAY LIFE

As well as socializing with people and other animals, a young puppy needs to become familiar with all the sights, smells, sounds and events that are part of our everyday life. Puppies need to be comfortable with household events, such as visitors arriving, vacuuming, dustbin collection and the phone ringing, if they are to live easily as pets in our homes. They also need to get used to a wide variety of everyday experiences, such as bus or car travel, walks in the town and country, and visits to the vet.

Why is socialization important?

Shy dogs are often less successful as pets since they are not as friendly with strangers and are not happy when taken out. Dogs that are not socialized with people will be scared of them and worried when they approach. This fear can rapidly develop into aggression. Dogs that have not been well socialized as puppies with other dogs will not have the necessary social skills for successful encounters with them, and they may get into fights more often.

A puppy that has only limited access to home life and to the outside world will be on edge and frightened when it is taken to new places. Outings with shy dogs are likely to be a trial for both the dog and its owner.

When should socialization begin?

A puppy's senses begin to operate at around three weeks. Gradually it begins to take in information about the world. Up until the age of about 12 weeks, it will be relatively fearless, but after this time it becomes increasingly wary of anything new. For this reason, the ideal time to socialize a puppy is between three and 12 weeks of age when it will take new

Right: Learning how to interact with other dogs is an essential for pet dogs, and social skills are learnt most easily during puppyhood.

Right: It is unwise to buy a puppy that is older than eight weeks unless he has been well socialized with humans.

things in its stride and will rapidly become confident and outgoing. Familiarization with humans, other animals and things in the environment should then continue until the puppy is one year old so that all the good early work can be maximized.

If a puppy has missed out on early socialization, it is possible to make up for lost time, but this becomes increasingly difficult as the puppy gets older. Such puppies may always remain shy in certain situations.

Buying a puppy

It is important to acquire your puppy from a breeder who has taken care to rear their puppies in a home environment and who has made every effort to maximize their development. Never be tempted to buy a puppy from someone who will deliver him or who has numerous litters of puppies, often from different breeds, for sale.

It is also unwise to buy a puppy older than eight weeks unless he has been kept separately from other dogs and learned to relate well to people. A puppy that has spent a long time playing with other dogs rather than people can be less than ideal as an adult.

Bringing your puppy home

When you get your puppy home, implement a gradually increasing schedule of events designed to expose him to people, other animals and environments. Socializing a puppy and taking him out and about to experience new situations is not difficult but does require sustained effort while he is young. Try to do something different each day; he should meet at least one new adult or child and have a good experience with them.

Below: Take particular care if your puppy is shy or sensitive, and give him more opportunities to overcome his fears.

TAKE IT GRADUALLY

Do not overwhelm your puppy with too much too soon. Watch him to see whether he is enjoying new events and taking them in his stride. If he looks anxious, slow down and give him time to overcome his concerns. Think ahead and prevent any unpleasant experiences. Do a small amount of socialization several times each day so that your puppy does not become tired. Gradually, as he grows, you will be able to do more and can begin to include him in your daily life more.

AN ONGOING PROCESS

Socialize your puppy until he has become a mature adult to ensure that he remains friendly and interested in people throughout his life. If his early life is happy, he will grow up with a view of the world as a safe and comfortable place. This will allow him to be friendly and outgoing.

Right: If your puppy will not read the signs that the other dogs give, help out by physically restraining him until he learns how to behave.

TRAINING OLDER DOGS

The old saying that 'you can't teach an old dog new tricks' is simply not true. One of the requirements of a hunting/scavenging existence is that you need to be adaptable. This trait has been handed down to our domestic dogs and they remain flexible in their behaviour and open to change throughout their lives.

If you choose an adult dog rather than a puppy it is still possible to channel unacceptable behaviour into more acceptable avenues, and new behaviour patterns

Above: The result of a lack of early socialization. Despite a caring owner, this dog remains afraid and is reluctant to approach or be friendly with strangers.

Left: Older dogs may take more time to learn new ways because you will be working against established behaviour patterns. However, all dogs will readily pick up new ways of behaving if it is to their advantage to do so.

can be developed. All you need is an understanding of why dogs do what they do and a knowledge of the training principles given later in this book.

Be realistic

Although it is relatively easy to change the way in which a dog behaves, it is unlikely that you will be able to change a dog's character fundamentally once he is mature. A shy, submissive dog, for example, is unlikely to become a super-confident extrovert.

Being realistic about how much you can change the way your dog behaves is important, but, with knowledge, understanding and some effort, even the most unruly of dogs can be tamed eventually.

COMMUNICATING WITH YOUR DOG

The reason why dogs make such popular pets is that they are so like us in many ways, but this can often deceive us into thinking that they are just like us in all ways – a less complicated, furry version of ourselves or our children. We may expect them to think and act like small people. They cannot. All they can be are dogs.

What is frequently overlooked is that they are members of a completely different species and, as such, often have surprising differences which can be the cause of problems between us. Understanding what dogs can and cannot do, and knowing their physical and mental limitations, is essential to having realistic expectations about their abilities.

Left: Dogs are not humans in furry skins but members of a completely different species.

THEIR PHYSICAL WORLD

It may seem too obvious to say that dogs experience things at a different level to us. But imagine what it must be like to live in a world where you cannot see the faces of the animals you live with when they walk around and where most of the interesting things they do, such as eating, take place way above your head. Getting down to your dog's level and looking at things from his perspective will give you a surprisingly different view of the world that we both inhabit.

Right: Dogs need to adapt their behaviour when living in a world designed for humans. They are smaller than us and see things from a different perspective. Living in a world where you are often too small to see what is going on must be frustrating.

A DOG'S SENSES

A dog's senses are different from ours. They have an incredible sense of smell and live in a more scent-oriented world. Their hearing is more acute and they are able to locate sound sources more accurately.

Paws and jaws

It may seem obvious, but dogs have no opposable thumb. This means they cannot pick up objects easily with their paws and, instead, will often use their mouths in situations where we would use our hands.

Dogs do not hit people when upset but bite instead. They learn to be very accurate with their mouths and, once experienced, will only rarely make unintentional contact with their teeth on human skin. In other words, if a dog snaps but misses, he probably meant to! Dogs will also explore using their mouths in the same way as we will touch unusual objects.

Right: Smells on the ground usually need careful investigation.

Another striking difference between our species is that, as primates, we like to touch, hold, hug and cuddle to express affection. However, dogs rarely do this to each other unless they are fighting or mating. This accounts for why some dogs will bite when hugged or stroked, especially by children. In order for dogs to accept our loving behaviour, they need to become accustomed to it gradually, preferably in puppyhood.

Super scenting

One of the first things that a dog will do in a new environment is to put his nose to the floor and sniff; a human in the same situation would look around. A dog meeting another dog or a person will, characteristically, sniff them, sometimes in the most embarrassing, but smelliest, places; a human will just look.

Both are gathering information about their world, but the way in which they do it illustrates an important difference between them. We live in a very visual world, whereas dogs live in a very smelly one.

Above: Dogs gather a lot of information by sniffing at places in a territory which have been marked by other dogs.

A MORE DEVELOPED SENSE OF SMELL

Dogs' sense of smell is incredible by our standards. Not only do they have many more cells in their nose for detecting different smells (the area used for smell detection is fourteen times the size of ours), but these cells are of better quality and the part of their brain that receives the information is more developed. This allows dogs to detect and identify a much wider variety of scents at lower concentrations.

Using this ability enables them to acquire much more information in one sniff than we can ever imagine. Information such as sex, health and social standing may be passed on through urine and faeces allowing males, and some females, to advertise their presence and status by marking lamp-posts and clumps of grass.

Although we cannot even begin to understand what it is like to be able to detect odours in this way, knowing that dogs live in a different sensory world can help us to understand them better and explain some of their habits, such as sniffing everything they come into contact with, kicking up earth with their back hind legs after going to the toilet (they have scent glands in between their pads), and rolling in smelly substances.

Above: Most male adolescent dogs will spend a lot of time sniffing and marking their territory.

Sensitive sight

Dogs can see less well than humans. They can see colours but not as well as we can, and they cannot differentiate easily between certain colours, such as red and green. A dog looking for a red ball on green grass is more likely to be using his nose than his eyes.

Dogs see better than us when less light is available. A reflective layer at the back of their eyes traps and reuses it. This is why their eyes shine eerily when they are caught in car headlights or a torch beam.

Whereas we are able to make out static shapes easily and can differentiate quickly between two objects, dogs see things better when they move, helping them to be efficient hunters. They notice even subtle body movements and can detect, a fraction of a second before we have said anything, that we are about to take them for a walk.

Left: Breeds with hair that hangs over their eyes will have their field of vision greatly reduced. It should be clipped or tied up out of the way.

Dogs have a greater field of vision than us. This enables them to see things to the rear and sides. The amount of overlap (shaded area) will determine how well the animal can judge distances.

Left and above: A whippet's field of vision is about 200 degrees.

Below: Dogs that have been bred to look more like us, such as the King Charles Spaniel, with forward-facing eyes, have a reduced field of vision.

Impressive hearing

Dogs can hear better than we can. A sound that can just be heard by a person 100 metres away, can be heard by a dog for up to 450 metres. They can also hear sounds of a higher frequency. Our range is up to about 20 kHz whereas dogs can hear sounds up to at least 35 kHz, allowing them to hear in the ultrasonic range. They also seem to be able to discriminate between two sounds that appear the same to us.

A SIXTH SENSE

It is probably this sense more than any other that has led people to believe that dogs have a 'sixth' sense. Because of their superior hearing, they may become aware of the arrival of their owner long before a person sitting in the same room. A dog can hear things that we

Left: Dogs with long, fluffy ears, such as the Cocker Spaniel, are likely to be less good at sound detection and location.

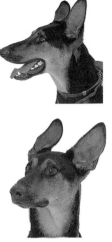

Above and right: Dogs can locate a sound source more accurately than us. This is achieved by having ears that can be manoeuvred into a position that allows them to catch sound more efficiently.

cannot, such as a 'silent' dog whistle, and may alert us to the presence of intruders or other noises in the environment long before we have heard anything.

Sound sensitivity

Dogs that were once used for herding, such as collies, have very sensitive hearing and, as a result, are more likely to find it difficult to live in noisy environments. They are also more prone than other dogs to developing noise phobias.

DOGS' BODY LANGUAGE

Everyday communication between adult dogs relies mostly on body posture and scent exchange with little in the way of vocalization. In comparison, we rely heavily on the spoken (or written) word and only use body signals and scent in subtle and secondary ways.

Body language versus spoken word

Knowing no better, dogs assume that our methods of communication are similar to their own and will attempt to communicate using body postures and signals. Owners need to know what to look for so that they do not miss these vital signs from their pets.

Dogs also watch our body language to find out what we want them to do. This is why they learn hand/arm signals more quickly than spoken commands. Pointing out the direction you want your dog to take by using an obvious arm and hand movement, is surprisingly effective, especially once he has become familiar with the signal. If, for example, he has just brought a recently unearthed bone in from the garden and is about to drop it on the carpet, shouting at him to go out may not be effective. Asking him to go out, leading the way and pointing out the direction you intend him to take with a clear hand and arm movement, will give him a more obvious message.

PLAYBOW

The universal invitation to play. A sudden drop into this position usually results in a frantic bout of tag between two playful dogs. If directed at a human, the dog is asking if you would like to play a game with him.

Right: The playbow is an obvious invitation to play.

FEARFUL DOG

Frightened dogs will have a lot of their weight on their back legs ready to run. Their head is held high ready for a defensive bite if necessary. They hold their tail low or tucked in, ears drawn back but not pinned flat against the head. They will often pant in short, sharp breaths and may yawn a lot.

In extreme cases, or if the dog is afraid for too long, they may begin to shake or tremble. The whites of their eyes can be seen as their eyes are held as wide open as possible. The pupils are often wide open and consequently the eyes may have a reddish tinge. If the eyes appear red and glassy, the dog is very fearful and should be approached with caution as he may well bite in self defence.

The hair along the back of the neck (the hackles) and the spine may also be raised, especially if he is fearful of other dogs. These make him look larger than he is and help to reduce the chances of him being attacked.

Left: A frightened dog holding its tail low between its legs.

Dogs that are anxious but not yet very fearful will exhibit some or all of these signs in varying degrees. Watching for subtle clues that your dog is ill-at-ease can help you to take the appropriate action and may prevent your dog from becoming scared or aggressive.

CONFIDENT DOG

A confident dog will hold his head and tail up and his body erect, proudly displaying strength and purpose. He will often have a 'presence' which encourages you to pay attention to him and appears very self assured. Very confident dogs rarely use aggression to get their own way since they are sure of their ability to do so without using force. Less confident dogs are less sure of their abilities and may resort to confrontation if they think they will lose. Confident dogs will have had many successful encounters with others and are often good at communication.

Right: This confident dog has an erect posture with head and tail held high.

SUBMISSIVE DOG

A submissive dog will make himself as vulnerable as possible to deter attack from a stronger member of the pack. By appeasing gestures, such as lip licking, he is more likely to be tolerated by stronger dogs.

SUBMISSIVE GRIN

This greeting looks ferocious but is, actually, totally harmless. The submissive grin is seen more often in specific breeds, such as the Dalmatian, and seems to be their way of greeting important individuals. They will also grin in this way when told off, giving rise to the theory that it is a form of appeasement gesture.

Above: Adopting a submissive position helps to turn off aggression and signals an intent to appease.

HAPPY DOG

A dog that is pleased to see you will wag his tail, the rear half of his body as well sometimes, press his ears back to the sides of his head and pull the corners of his mouth back in greeting. Happy dogs appear relaxed; their bodies will be soft, not tense. They will eat readily and be happy to play games and be handled. A pet dog should be relaxed, calm and happy most of the time.

TAIL WAGGING

A wagging tail does not necessarily indicate friendly intent, but is a sign of an excited, aroused state. Happy dogs will wag their tails in a sweeping side-to-side motion. Frightened dogs will often hold their tails low with just the tip waggling. A confident dog about to bite will often hold his tail high and stiffly wagging.

Right: A wagging tail can trick people into thinking the dog is pleased to see them whereas it may mean only that the dog is excited.

ANGRY DOG

An angry dog will often become very still and stiff just before he bites. This gives him time to weigh up the opposition and gives the opponent a chance to back down or submit. If you find yourself in a situation where you have done something to make a dog react in this way, for example, you have stroked a dog that did not want to be touched, be very careful what you do next. Keep very still, look away and retreat very slowly. The signs to look for are as follows:

- Stillness and a rigid posture.
- Eyes fixed and staring.
- Conflicting signals of confidence and fear, such as the tail held high, head high, eyes wide and pupils dilated, hackles raised.

When a dog becomes angry, adrenalin flows around the body and other changes occur that help to sustain

Watch and learn

Observation is a learned skill which can be developed by owners. Carefully watch what your dog does when meeting a stranger or another dog and try to interpret the reason behind even seemingly unimportant behaviour. Everything is done for a reason and, with practice, you should be able to identify why your dog does what he does in any given situation.

any action that may be taken. For this reason, it is always best to isolate an angry dog and to let him calm down for at least half an hour before you approach him again. If your dog has had a bad experience, he is likely to be more reactive for a few days after the incident so care should be taken until he has recovered.

Above: Territorial aggression is caused by fear of strangers entering the property. Threat displays at boundaries make it less likely that the intruder will enter, keeping the dog inside safe.

VOCAL COMMUNICATION

Words are relatively difficult for dogs to learn. They can learn to associate words with actions, but many repetitions are needed before they understand exactly what is required. It is not a natural communication method for them and, consequently, owners who rely solely on word commands will find it more difficult to communicate effectively with their dogs.

Using tone of voice

Dogs will determine our mood from our tone of voice. It is not so much what we say but the way we say it that is important. Try to modulate the way you say things to convey different moods more easily. For example, vary the tone of voice used to communicate how urgent a request is, how pleased you are or how angry you are. Dogs are fairly emotional beings and by communicating our feelings to them more readily, they will be better able to judge what we want from them.

Left: Teaching signals before teaching words will result in a faster response and less confusion for the dog.

VISUAL COMMUNICATION

A direct stare between dogs is often used to threaten or intimidate. Since humans often look lovingly into their pets' eyes, dogs need to get used to this. Most will look away and be uncomfortable if you continue to stare. Fearful dogs may growl or back away if you stare. Well-socialized dogs who are familiar with our eye contact may stare back happily and wag their tails.

Making eye contact

If you do not know a dog, avoid prolonged direct eye contact with him. Staring at your own dog may cause him discomfort, so avoid this. Get him accustomed to eye contact by showing him a titbit and holding it under your chin. Wait for him to look up into your eyes, then feed him the food. He will learn to look into your eyes to get the titbit. You can gradually increase the time he looks at you.

Right: Even loving stares from an owner can make a dog feel uncomfortable.

DISPLACEMENT BEHAVIOUR

When dogs feel under pressure or uncomfortable about something, they may carry out a seemingly unrelated, unimportant behaviour, such as yawning, scratching or sniffing. This seems to help them to relieve the anxiety they are feeling and provides a temporary relief from the tension. If your dog does this a lot, try to identify what it is that triggers the behaviour. If it is something that you do, you may like to either stop doing it or try to make him feel more comfortable about it in future.

Appeasement gestures

Dogs will use a variety of appeasement gestures in response to individuals whom they consider to be higher in status than themselves. These gestures may take the form of lip licking (their own), skin licking (ours), particularly of the face and mouth, rolling over to expose their vulnerable areas, turning the head away and avoiding direct eye contact, and urinating.

Left: Yawning helps to release some of the tension this dog feels.

UNDERSTANDING THE GESTURES

Appeasement gestures help to pacify the dominant individuals in the pack and reassure them of their status, making it less likely that the subordinate will be attacked. Puppies, juveniles and individuals that consider themselves to be of low status are more likely to display such gestures. Any punishment given by humans in an effort to try to stop these behaviours is likely to have the opposite effect as the dog tries even harder to appease. Understanding these gestures and attempting to rebuild the dog's confidence and trust are more likely to succeed.

Below: A combination of words and signals will enable your dog to learn commands more easily.

ENCOURAGING GOOD BEHAVIOUR

Achieving a good relationship between yourself and your dog is very important. A bond of friendship and trust between you will lead to good behaviour and harmony. To achieve this, take the initiative and act in a way that promotes a successful alliance.

Left: Praise from an owner who is also a best friend will always mean a lot to a pet dog.

MAKE YOUR DOG WANT TO PLEASE YOU

You can make your dog do what you say, but he will do it reluctantly and because he has to. A dog that does things willingly is more rewarding. This is only possible if he genuinely wants to please you because you are his best friend. The secret lies in making good behaviour advantageous to him. Owners who can empathize with their dogs are more successful in achieving good behaviour. Owners who think only of themselves, and what they want, are less successful.

Reward good behaviour

Whenever your dog does something you approve of, it is important to let him know. If you are his friend, your praise will mean a lot to him. Give him positive feedback whenever he does something right. This will make him feel happy about doing it and he is more likely to do it again. In this way, good behaviour is promoted and is more likely to happen in future.

It is surprising how many owners will reprimand their dog for bad behaviour but ignore him when he is good. Some dogs become so desperate for attention that they prefer being told off to being ignored and their behaviour begins to deteriorate. Always reward good behaviour even if your dog is not drawing attention to himself. When he is lying down quietly,

Above: A good relationship between you and your dog is more fulfilling for both parties.

gently praise him. This will make it more likely that he does it more often. Waiting until he is bored and has begun to chew or whine for attention before responding will make the unwanted behaviour more frequent.

Being affectionate and providing an environment where you live in harmony will contrast with times when you may need to reprimand your dog. If a dog has an adversarial relationship with his owner, being told off will be nothing new, but for a dog whose relationship is based on friendship, being told off is a very big deal.

Error-free learning

Try to manage situations and engineer events so that your dog does the right thing most of the time. This will allow you to be generally positive and rewarding. For example, instead of leaving a young dog alone in the house with nothing to do, provide suitable toys and chews and ensure that he has had a long walk beforehand to tire him out. This will make it less likely that he will get into trouble by chewing things he should not. Providing situations where your dog learns to do the right thing from the outset will be a lot easier than allowing him to get into bad habits which you will then need to break.

Below: Providing a variety of interesting chews and changing these every few days will help prevent your puppy chewing things that you would rather he did not.

PREVENT UNWANTED BEHAVIOUR

Think ahead to prevent potential trouble. If you know that your dog has a tendency to jump up on visitors as they arrive, put him on a lead or hold onto his collar before opening the door to prevent him from doing so. Physically preventing unwanted behaviour using gentle restraint via a collar and lead will allow good behaviour to happen which can be rewarded.

Above: Prevent unwanted behaviour by gentle restraint.

Allowing too much freedom before you have achieved mental control will mean that your dog will be able to find his own reward in bad behaviour. If this happens, bad habits form that may be difficult to put right.

Don't shout!

Using punishment, scoldings or shouting as a way of stopping bad behaviour is ineffective. Such measures usually only cause your dog to become worried. Once he is anxious or afraid, he will not be in a good frame of mind to learn the correct way to behave. Rather than learning how to do the right thing, he learns how unpleasant his owner can sometimes become.

A QUESTION OF TRUST

When taken to extremes, threats or punishment can intimidate a dog to the point where he becomes frightened to do anything in case it is wrong. A dog that is frequently punished may live in fear of being attacked by his owners and may start biting to defend himself. Since the reason for punishment is not always clear, especially if the punishment takes place long after the event that provoked it, owners may appear, from the dog's point of view, unpredictably aggressive. If a dog cannot trust his owners, he is unlikely to trust other humans and, therefore, punishing a dog will make him more likely to bite other people in future.

Above: Your puppy will not see this as 'stealing'. Dogs are opportunists and will make the most of any situation they find themselves in.

RE-EVALUATE YOUR RELATIONSHIP

Constant scoldings and shouting can be unpleasant and stressful for the owner as well as the dog. They are unlikely to produce the desired response from the dog and will eventually destroy a good relationship. Shouting is a sign that the owner is out of control. Only weak, ineffective leaders shout; strong, efficient ones only have to make their requirements known to get compliance. In extreme cases, where the dog's desires are at odds with those of his owners, they need only raise their voice slightly to enforce their will. If you often feel the need to shout at your dog, it is probably time to re-evaluate your relationship and build a new one that is based on respect and friendship.

Don't punish after the event

Owners will often punish a dog that has done something wrong while he was left alone. Punishment after the event only serves to increase the dog's view of his owners as unpredictable. Dogs cannot learn from this as they cannot relate the punishment to the unwanted behaviour, even if taken to the scene of the crime. They can remember what they have done but cannot associate the punishment with their earlier behaviour.

Below: Punishing problem behaviour after the event will not prevent it in future.

Humans are fooled into thinking that they can because their dog will look 'guilty' when they return home, but this is a natural submissive reaction to the anger of a pack member of higher status. They may even learn to associate chewed items or mess on the floor with this response and begin to show submission before the owner has noticed something is amiss. This provides further evidence of their supposed 'guilt'. Punishing a dog after the event has no beneficial effect on preventing the behaviour when you are out in future. Again, all it serves to do is to weaken the relationship between you and your dog.

Prevent problems with other dogs

If dogs lived with other dogs all their lives, they would learn the social rules and body language necessary for peaceful encounters with unfamiliar dogs. Many pet dogs grow up with only humans in their family and this can lead to problem encounters and fighting with other dogs, especially during the adolescent period when hormone surges affect behaviour.

PUPPY CLASSES

To avoid problems later, your puppy should play with other friendly dogs as he grows up. You can take him to puppy classes from about 12 weeks onwards. A good trainer will allow only two or three selected puppies off lead at a time. This allows puppies with similar characters to play and gain confidence and prevents a free-for-all which frightens some and makes bullies of others.

PLAYING WITH ADULT DOGS

Your puppy should also play with friendly adult dogs. If he only comes into contact with other puppies, his boisterous play behaviour is likely to get him into trouble when he reaches maturity. Adult dogs that like puppies but will not tolerate them putting their teeth and paws all over them will help to teach them respect. These dogs will need to have been well socialized with other dogs and be used to puppies.

If you have another dog at home, it is still important that your puppy meets other dogs. This will help him to learn how to deal with different types of dogs.

Right: This adult dog makes it very clear that he does not want to play at this time. A well-socialized dog will help to teach your puppy respect without being aggressive.

BE A GOOD PACK LEADER

Dogs are often happier and better behaved if they have a strong, supportive leader to protect and guide them. This frees them from the responsibility of leadership, and they can relax and be playful, safe in the knowledge that someone is looking after them. Just like young children, dogs prefer to be given direction and guidance provided that it is not overbearing. Providing them with a framework of guidelines and clear boundaries allows them to be sure of their role while allowing them the freedom to be themselves. Being a good pack leader is not just about having the

Right: Taking on the pack leader role will allow your dogs to relax and feel safe.

Right: Your dog may challenge you but only respond if you are able to win.

right to make decisions. It is also about taking on the responsibility to protect pack members and ensure that their needs are provided for. Your job will be to keep your dog safe, deal with anything he may find threatening, and provide exercise, games, food and social contact. If you meet these requirements, your dog will want you as his pack leader and will be loyal and faithful, making dog ownership worthwhile.

Behaviour changes

As pack leaders, the way we are feeling will rub off on our dogs. If they are closely bonded to us, they will reflect our moods and be influenced by them. If we are anxious, happy, sad or lively, our dogs probably will be too – bear this in mind when you are anxious or stressed. Your dog is likely to pick up on this and become anxious or stressed, too. Watch out for subtle signs and be aware that behaviour changes in your dog may result from a behaviour change in you.

Living in a pack

An essential ingredient for all pack animals is to live in a hierarchy in which not all animals are equal. This reduces the risk of injury from fights between pack members by arranging animals in order of mental and physical strength. Fights only occur between animals of similar strength and are thus quite rare. Minimizing the fighting in this way is important when individuals possess such large teeth and strong jaws.

Animals at the top of the hierarchy are usually the biggest, strongest and most clever. They have a right of access to resources in preference to those beneath them. In years of famine, a hierarchy ensures that the strongest animals survive to produce the next generation, so competition for the top places is fierce.

ACHIEVING HIGH STATUS

Although diluted by the process of domestication, the desire for high status among our pet dogs is often very important and it is vital that we understand it. Achieving high status means more to some dogs than others but, overall, it is a process that is well worth considering when trying to live with a member of a different species in your home.

Having a dog that considers himself below all family members is essential for a harmonious existence. A dog that thinks he is in charge will be difficult to live with and will want to follow his own ideas instead of those of his owners. He is likely to be over-active, difficult to control, over-boisterous with visitors, and may be aggressive if he does not get his own way.

Left: Over a period of time, a natural hierarchy is established among a group of dogs that live together.

Having the right attitude

Getting the upper hand is not difficult and there is no need to resort to aggression yourself in order to achieve it. High status, and the respect that goes with it, is something that has to be earned. It is given by the subordinate rather than enforced by the leader. Resorting to punishment may lead to intimidation through fear, but is unlikely to lead to a freely-given respect for your authority – essential for a good relationship. Being a good pack leader is not about bullying others into submission but about making them want to have you as their leader.

Right: Strong leaders like to win games and are possessive over toys.

AN AIR OF AUTHORITY

One of the most important qualities for getting respect is to have an air of authority. You can achieve this by having the attitude that your dog will be reasonably well behaved and you will do whatever is necessary to achieve success during your encounters with him. Often it is not the big things that matter, but the smaller, everyday occurrences. Insist that your dog comes when you call him, or moves out of the way when you ask him. If there are lots of instances where you have won, and he has lost, over smaller issues, he is unlikely to risk bigger challenges as he will not be confident of winning. Having an attitude that allows you to win small contests will earn you respect.

Right: Giving periods of 'time out' will result in a dog that is content to leave you in peace sometimes rather than one that will demand your attention constantly.

Learning to lead the pack

In order to be a good pack leader, you need to know which resources your dog considers most important. You can then teach him that should you require access to these resources at any time, it is your right as pack leader to do so. This is very important when taking a puppy or a new adult dog into your pack.

Although you will not need to use these techniques all the time once you have attained leadership status, it is useful to know them so that you can settle a new dog or puppy into your pack more easily.

Left: At times you have to make it clear to your dog that you are in charge – not him.

Right: Make it clear that you own the territory and that your dog cannot always go where he wants to.

Knowledge of these techniques will also give you a greater understanding of your dog and will help you to appreciate why he behaves as he does in certain situations.

FOOD

It is the right of the dominant dog to eat first and have first choice of any available food. You should be seen to be in control of the food and it is up to you when you give it rather than feeding on demand.

Right: Food is a daily highlight so you choose when you want to give it to your dog.

Above: Your dog should get out of the chair immediately whenever you ask him to do so.

SLEEPING PLACES AND TERRITORY

It is the right of the dominant dog to sleep where he wants and to go to or rest in any part of the territory if he wants to. In order to achieve high status, be sure that you are able to remove your dog from the places you want to be whenever you want to be there. Ask him to move if he is blocking the way and, occasionally, ask him to move from where he was resting so that you can sit there yourself. Keep him off beds and chairs if it is difficult to remove him easily from them.

As the dominant animal, you should lead the pack and your dog should follow. Make sure this occurs when going through doorways or narrow passageways together. Those of higher status always go first.

Height advantage is also important to dogs and, with a new dog or a very pushy one, you should make sure you keep him below you. This applies to going up or down the stairs, or when you are sitting down.

TOYS AND POSSESSIONS

The dominant dog has the right to make use of any possession within his territory at any time. Usually, the possessions most important to dogs are their toys. To be a strong leader, it is important that you can

Right: Teaching your puppy to leave a toy on command is a useful exercise. Begin by offering incentives so that it is worth his while to give up playing his favourite game.

control games with toys and take possession of them yourself if you want to do so. Playing tug-of-war to win and maintaining possession of the toy at the end of the game is a good way to impress on your dog that you are strong enough to win if you want to.

AFFECTION AND SOCIAL CONTACT

A dominant dog has the right to initiate social interactions if he wishes or to ignore invitations from others if he does not want contact. Not responding to all your dog's requests for attention or affection, as well as beginning and ending social interactions with him to suit you, will confer high status.

When to say 'no' and mean it

Sometimes you must make it clear to your dog that you are in charge, and if his behaviour is really unacceptable you need to ensure it never happens again. At such times, you should use your voice to make it obvious that you are not happy. A deep, loud exclamation is powerful enough to stop your dog in his tracks. Back this up with physical restraint, holding his collar if necessary to stop the behaviour.

After such a correction, get him to do something you can be pleased about. Take him away from the area and ask him to sit or lie down if he knows the command. Praise him for responding. By providing a contrast between your responses to good and bad behaviour he will rapidly learn what he should and should not do.

ENSURING YOU WIN

If your dog is challenging you for status, you will need to make it very obvious that you are stronger than him. Only respond to a challenge if you are willing and able to carry it through and win, no matter what your dog may do. Alternatively, ignore the challenge and ensure that you win over smaller issues, particularly with regard to the resources he finds most important, to reduce his confidence. Work out a strategy to maintain control should a similar challenge arise in future.

Right: Rewards in the form of tasty titbits and gentle praise make it more likely that your dog will repeat good behaviour.

THE WELL-BEHAVED DOG

A contented dog is a good dog. Dogs that do not have everything they need behave in ways that make it possible for them to achieve those needs. These are often unacceptable to us and at odds with how we want our dogs to be. To overcome this, we must provide all their essential needs so they are contented and can relax and behave in an acceptable way.

Their essential needs are not much different from ours, but many owners do not consider that their dogs have any other than physical needs. Keeping their bodies healthy is just one aspect of good dog ownership. Keeping their minds content is a different task.

Left: A happy dog has an owner who caters for all his essential needs.

ESSENTIAL NEEDS

These originate from when dogs lived as wild animals. To fulfil them, they behave in certain ways. Although they no longer need to show all these behaviours for survival, they still retain the capacity and desire to do so.

• A need to be safe.
• A need to maintain their bodies.
• A need to reproduce.
• A need for social contact.

Feeling safe

In the wild, if a dog does not stay safe, he is likely to be injured or killed. This is why feeling safe takes precedence over everything else for pet dogs. If your dog is stressed or frightened, he will show a range of unwanted behaviours to make himself feel more secure.

Dogs get scared of unfamiliar things which appear, to them, to pose a risk to themselves or their pack. They may be frightened of certain people, children, other dogs, things on wheels, vacuum cleaners or noises. Fear often manifests itself in excessive barking or aggression, but it can cause dogs to be quiet and unresponsive.

SOLVING THE PROBLEM

Understanding that your dog is fearful, even if he is displaying overt aggression, is essential. Dogs that feel safe in their own world are unlikely to show these unwanted behaviours; there is no need to do so. Keeping your dog safe from things that frighten him, or helping him to overcome his fear by gradual exposure to low levels of whatever it is that scares him, will help him to feel safer. By keeping fear levels low and making new encounters fun, the problem can be gradually overcome.

Left: An open indoor kennel can become a safe den when covered by a thick blanket and placed in a quiet corner.

Right: Dogs that are worried often find it difficult to cope when they are left alone by their owners.

HOME ALONE

When a dog finds himself alone, feeling safe is very important. Dogs that feel unsafe may try a range of behaviours to make themselves feel more secure. They may attempt to get to their owners, causing damage to doors and windows or chew things that their owners have recently touched or worn. They may try to dig themselves a den, usually in a sofa or mattress, or mark strategic points with urine to deter anything that may decide to come in while their owners are away.

Isolation is not a natural state for a dog. Gradually accustoming your dog to being left alone so that he feels safe when you leave him is essential to good behaviour. Providing him with a small covered area resembling a den to hide in, and giving him an item of clothing which smells of you when you leave will also help him to feel safe in your absence.

Staying fit

Our pet dogs need to keep fit and to acquire food in order to maintain their bodies in good condition. We provide them with enough food for their daily needs, but they have not lost the desire to exercise. If they had to hunt for their food they would need to run, jump, chase, capture, chew and dig to bury the excess.

Providing sufficient physical and mental exercise to fulfil these needs is essential if your dog is to be content. Exercising your dog's body only is never enough;

Above: Playing with toys is an excellent way to improve your relationship and use up excess energy.

Above: Active games with toys can tire the dog's mind as well as his body.

exercising his mind is also required. It is essential that most of his hunting behaviour is diverted into play with toys and other acceptable activities.

EXERCISING YOUR DOG

The amount of exercise a dog needs depends on the individual. Genetics have an important influence, as does age. Younger dogs from working strains or breeds that were required to run or work all day will have plenty of energy and require more exercise. Older dogs or those from breeds designed to be lap dogs will require less exercise. Dogs with bodies that are dictated by fashion to be impractical will not be able to exercise very much without becoming exhausted.

Above: Collies have enough energy to run all day long.

It is important to provide the right amount of physical exercise. The consequences of not doing this are obvious: excess energy is likely to be channelled into unwanted behaviour, such as over-zealous greeting of owners or visitors, attention-seeking, or boisterous play with toys. Dogs with too much energy often get banished to the garden where they annoy the neighbours with excessive barking.

WALK YOUR DOG REGULARLY

Taking your dog out for walks allows him to use up his energy. Ideally, he should be walked at least twice a day – morning and evening. This allows him to go to the toilet and exercise physically and mentally. Dogs that are walked away from their homes on a regular basis are less likely to be territorial and are probably more sociable with other animals and people.

The length of time you need to spend out on walks will depend on your dog's energy level. If he shows unwanted behaviour in the house, you will need to step up the amount he is exercised until you reach a level that suits him. You can increase the amount of exercise he gets on each walk by playing games with him.

Remember to take his toys out with you rather than playing with sticks which can injure him. You can also increase the amount of exercise he gets by letting him off the lead to run free. For all dogs, freedom off the lead to run and play is essential. Ensure that your dog is under control, by teaching him to come back reliably when called (see page 102).

Right: Jogging with your dog will keep both of you fit and you will both be more relaxed at home.

A need to reproduce

In a wolf pack, only those at the top of the hierarchy are likely to breed so achieving high status is very important. The ambition to be the top dog has been retained to a lesser extent in our pet dogs, although more so in some than others. Impressing on your dog that his place is at the bottom of the pack will satisfy him that he has done all he can to get as high as he can and he will, hopefully, give up trying.

COMPETING FOR STATUS

Competition for the right to breed can be a problem if two or more uncastrated males or unspayed females are kept together. If they have similar strengths of character, they may compete between themselves. This is very noticeable during seasons in females and whenever males can smell the scent of a bitch on heat.

If bitches are kept together, it is advisable to have them spayed to eliminate problems when they are in season (or on heat). Since males do not have seasons and are competing with each other throughout the year, it may be beneficial to neuter the weaker of the two dogs as this opens up a larger gap between them in status. Although this goes against the desire of owners to treat them both equally, it is better for the dogs so they can accept their positions more easily.

THE DESIRE TO MATE

This is stronger in some dogs than others. Some males will pace up and down, lose weight and make frantic attempts to get to bitches in season. Dogs with a strong desire to mate will often compete with other males in the neighbourhood, will mark their territory and spend a lot of time sniffing lamp-posts and other dogs.

They will often try to escape and spend time roaming, looking for a mate. They may also attempt to mount bedding, stuffed toys, children or people's legs. Such dogs may benefit from being castrated. This relatively simple operation can save them years of frustration and removes the unwanted behaviour caused by hormones.

Right: Well socialized dogs will use play rather than fighting in order to determine who will have a higher status in the relationship.

The need for social contact

In order to be safe, eat and reproduce, dogs need to be part of a social group. In the wild, being a member of a pack is a fundamental requirement for staying safe and healthy. Our pet dogs also need to feel they are closely associated with the other members of their pack, and, since they often live only with people, staying friends with their human family is very important to them.

PROVIDING LOVE AND ATTENTION

This may seem an obvious task but for many owners, the role of their pet dog is to provide them with love and attention, not the other way around. Some are just too busy caring for other family members, particularly if they have young children, to have anything left for their dog. Deprived of good-quality love and attention, a dog becomes desperate to get a response of any kind and can resort to disruptive and troublesome behaviour, such as attention seeking, escaping to find social contact elsewhere and howling to reunite it with its owners when separated.

Try to provide your dog with at least five minutes that you set aside just for him several times a day. This may not seem like much, and you can certainly give more time if you have it, but your undivided attention will mean a great deal to him. During this time you can stroke him, talk to him or give him whatever kind of attention he finds most enjoyable. The important thing is to make him feel loved and wanted. He needs to know that you are not doing it as a chore but that you genuinely want to spend time with him.

This will help him to feel connected to you and that he is part of the pack. It will allow him to feel safe and secure and will help prevent many of the unwanted behaviours that occur when dogs feel isolated and distanced from their pack.

Above: Spending quality time with your dog throughout the day will help him feel part of the family pack.

BASIC TRAINING

A popular misconception is that, as the owner, you have the right to expect obedience from your dog. However, dogs do not come ready programmed to obey. They are opportunistic individuals and will do whatever is to their advantage at any given moment. If we want them to do as we ask, we not only need to teach them the commands for certain actions but must also make it worthwhile for them to comply.

Right: Dogs are happy to learn if it is in their interests to do so.

WHY USE REWARDS?

The fundamental principle behind learning in all animals is that behaviour and actions that are rewarded will happen more often. A dog that has overturned a dustbin and found something tasty inside, for example, is likely to do it again, or a dog that jumps up and is given attention is likely to do so whenever he greets someone he likes. In a similar way, words associated with rewarding experiences are also remembered. Think how quickly a dog learns the word 'walkies!' or 'biscuit!'. If we can get that kind of enthusiasm associated with the words 'down' or 'come here' by using rewards, training will be easy.

Once your dog knows the commands, he will be happy to work for just your praise if he has a good relationship with you. However, in the early stages of training when he does not know what you want, he will have to work harder to comply with your requests.

Even once your dog knows your signals, there will be times when your requests are in direct conflict with what he wants to do (for example, if you have just called him when he is playing with another dog). At these times, the value of the reward you are offering needs to be higher than the rewards he would get if he did what he wanted to do.

MOTIVATING YOUR DOG

To make it easier for you to encourage your dog to comply with your requests, you will need to know what motivates him. Although there are several common areas of interest, dogs are all individuals and what interests one may not interest another. Finding out what your dog really likes from the list below is necessary before you can begin training:

• Praise and attention
• Food
• Games and play
• Movement

Below: Children are often very good at motivating dogs as they are enthusiastic, genuine and uninhibited.

Right: Many pet dogs can get attention from their owners any time they want it and thus are unlikely to work hard to earn it.

Praise and attention

If you are part of your dog's pack, he will want to stay friends with you. If you are of a higher status, he will choose to obey because he will have respect for you. The higher he perceives your status to be, the more likely it is that he will comply with your requests. If you find it difficult to keep control and he is often disobedient, even though you think he knows the signals, you may need to increase your status (see page 70).

If you have a good relationship with your dog, he will want to please you and will enjoy your praise and attention. You should remember, however, that pet dogs often get lots of praise and attention just for being there and, because of this, they may not be as willing to work for it. If you are constantly giving your dog attention because you want to, you will need to use other inducements to get him to work for you. Alternatively, you may like to reduce the amount of free attention you give and ask your dog to do something to earn it in future. There are several ways to give attention. It is important to choose the one that your dog enjoys the most.

TALKING

Praise your dog in a high-pitched, happy tone of voice. Let him know you are genuinely pleased when he has done something right and make this tone of voice very different from any other that you use. Be unrestrained and extravagant in your praise so that he is left in no doubt that he has pleased you.

Below: Some dogs like to be touched but stroke their bodies rather than their heads.

Right: Keeping a supply of treats around the house will enable you to do many short training sessions.

LOOKING

Some dogs enjoy direct eye contact more than others. If it makes your dog feel uncomfortable, do not stare at him while you praise him; look at his tail instead.

TOUCHING

Some dogs will like to be touched more than others. If your dog finds it rewarding, then make contact with him when he has done something right. Dogs have different body sensitivities and preferences so it is important to find out how and where your dog likes to be touched.

Some will prefer you not to touch their heads but will like to be stroked under the chin. Others will prefer to be touched along the back. Most dogs enjoy being stroked on the chest area. Whether you pat, stroke or tickle should be decided by your dog.

Food

Most dogs can be motivated by food, especially those with large appetites, such as Labradors. They do not have to be hungry, although it is advisable if training sessions coincide with times when your dog is about to be fed. The amount of food given needs to be small so that he does not become full too quickly. The more smelly and tasty the food, the more interested he will be. Dried food is most convenient to use.

Your dog may become bored with the treats you use after a while. Change to something else and you should see an improvement. Using a variety of different treats on a regular basis will help to prevent this problem.

Below: Toys are only rewarding if you use them to play a game.

Above: Games should be fun for both you and your puppy. If you are getting bored, stop, try a new toy or game to play.

Games and play

One of the best ways to motivate your dog to do things for you is through games. If your dog is having fun he is more likely to remember the lessons. Choose the game your dog likes the most (see page 120) and use it to encourage and reward the desired action.

Movement

Although it is difficult to use as a reward for the desired behaviour, movement is often intrinsically rewarding to dogs, especially young, energetic ones. Being allowed to run free or move forward rather than stand still will be rewarding for them.

SHORT TRAINING SESSIONS

Aim to train in short sessions of less than five minutes' duration. Several of these throughout the day on walks and at home, perhaps while you wait for the kettle to boil or a during commercial break, will soon result in a well-trained dog. As the sessions will be short, your dog will stay interested and keen to work. Long sessions result in tired, bored dogs and owners.

Below: Training can be difficult and frustrating for dogs too sometimes so give them frequent breaks for play.

Before training sessions, you should ensure that your dog is not exercised too much or too little and has had the opportunity to go to the toilet. At the end of each session, you should see some progress in terms of what your dog has learned. If not, think carefully about what you are trying to teach him and the way you are doing it. Training a dog requires lots of thought by the owner to achieve success.

Do not get angry

If you cannot get your dog to do what you want, you may get frustrated. Anger is a natural consequence of frustration. If you find yourself becoming angry, then ask your dog to do something that you know he can do so that you can reward him and immediately end the training session. Take time to calm down and think about what is going wrong so that your dog is more likely to get it right next time. And do not forget that dogs, like us, have days when they are feeling off colour. If your dog is not on top form, give him a rest and resume training the next day.

Reward right action

Dogs will not be able to concentrate or learn as quickly if they are stressed or worried. This is why it is important not to punish them in any way if they do not get things right. Just ignore incorrect moves or prevent them with some gentle restraint, and be sure to reward the right action.

TEACHING WORDS AND SIGNALS

Teaching a command can be broken down into three parts. You need to do the following:

- Get your dog to do the required action.
- Reward the desired action so it is more likely to happen in future.
- Associate a command with the required action.

Getting the required action

Lure your dog into position using a reward, or position the reward so that he has to perform the required action to get it. He will think about the situation and come up with the idea of what to do all by himself. As he begins to understand what is required, conceal the reward so that it is not an obvious enticement. He will become less fixated on the reward and more likely to pay attention to signals you give. Eventually, dispense with the lure as he responds to the signal only.

POSITIONING THE DOG

This method leaves the dog no choice but to carry out the behaviour, but it is often slower because the dog is not thinking for himself but is distracted by the feeling of being pushed or pulled. If too much force is used, or he is apprehensive of being handled, it may cause him anxiety and interfere with his ability to learn.

TIMING

Dogs live in the present, not in the past or future, and they will need to be rewarded for good behaviour immediately rather than later. They can remember what they have done but, without language, we cannot specify which particular behaviour the reward is for. Therefore, to make any difference to their future actions, rewards have to be given at once. Even more than two seconds later is too late because your dog will already be thinking of something else. For the best results, reward your dog with praise as soon as he begins the required action and back this up with other rewards as he completes it.

Right: At first, reward your dog as soon as his bottom touches the floor when asked to sit. Once he understands what is required, you can gradually ask him to wait for longer before rewarding him.

Putting the action on command

Once you are able to get your dog to do the desired action, put it on cue so that it will happen when you signal. To do this, all that is necessary is to signal to your dog just before the required action occurs so that he can associate it with the desired response.

For example, if you are teaching your dog to sit and have been luring him into position so that he will sit whenever you raise a titbit above his head, you will need to begin saying 'sit' just before you begin to raise the titbit. He will then begin to associate the word with the action of putting his bottom on the floor.

PRACTICE MAKES PERFECT

Many repetitions will be necessary before your dog anticipates what you require and he begins to do the action before being lured into position. When he begins to understand what you mean, leave a slightly longer gap between the signal and luring him into position to give him time to act on his own.

Associations

When your dog begins to work out what to do in order to get the reward, he will learn a set of associations surrounding the event. If you change any of these he will need to be taught the lesson from the beginning again. Thus if you teach him to sit in the kitchen and then take him to the garden and ask him to sit, he will not necessarily know what you mean.

This happens because your dog has learned a response to a set of associations, such as standing in front of you, the signal for 'sit' and being in the kitchen. In order to overcome this, you must teach him the lesson from the beginning in many different places and in many different positions until he begins to link the action to the signal only.

Above: Continue the training in different places with varying levels of distraction until you have a reliable response.

COME WHEN CALLED

Coming back when called is an essential command that will enable you to call your dog away from danger once you let him off the lead. It is one of the most useful commands a pet dog ever learns. Having a dog that reliably comes when called allows you to give him more freedom and exercise. This will make him more contented and, ultimately, better behaved.

1 Get someone to hold your dog by his collar. Show him that you have something that he wants.

When not to call

Never call your dog when you want to do something with him that he may find unpleasant, such as bathing him, cutting his nails or shutting him away from company, as it will make him less willing to respond next time. Always go and collect him instead.

2 Now run backwards, stop and crouch down facing him. Call him enthusiastically while opening your arms in a welcoming gesture (at this point, your helper should release his collar).

3 As he comes towards you, praise him in high, squeaky tones. As he gets closer, offer him the reward and use it to lure him right up to you. Before giving the reward, hold on to his collar. Give the reward but, before letting go of his collar, praise him enthusiastically and let him know he has done well.

WALKING ON A LEAD

This is essential since dogs that pull on the lead are unpleasant to take out. Dogs that are a pleasure to walk are taken out more frequently and get more exercise.

How to stop pulling

Move forward only when the lead is slack and stop when the lead is taut. This sounds simple, but is often the opposite of what happens. Dogs rapidly learn that leaning into the collar causes their owner to move forward. From there, walking on a lead easily falls into a pattern of the dog pulling and the owner moving forward. Owners often check their dog when they get fed up, which results in the dog temporarily giving up the struggle, but he soon begins to pull again.

Left: Teaching a dog to walk on a loose lead takes time and patience but it is well worth it in the end.

Rewarding good behaviour

There is no need to give any other rewards since the movement of going forward is a reward in itself. It may take a long time to get your dog to walk without pulling initially, but you will progress faster as he begins to learn what is required and break with old habits. He is likely to forget himself when he gets excited, but go back to your new routine if he pulls and he will soon learn it is not in his interests to do so.

Equipment

You need a strong buckle collar. Attach a lead which, if your dog were standing beside you with it clipped to his collar, would allow you to hold the handle against your stomach while the rest of the lead falls in a loop not quite reaching the floor.

USING A HEAD COLLAR

Only walk a puppy on a lead and collar when you have time to train him. When you cannot concentrate on him, get him used to wearing a head collar which is more effective at preventing him from pulling.

Right: A head collar is useful if you own a strong dog who pulls hard.

1 Stand still, holding the handle of the lead into your stomach with both hands. If your dog pulls into the lead, give it short, sharp tugs so that he cannot rely on it to lean against. This will make him stand up straight rather than lean into the lead. Do not say anything as this will break the concentration. Once he is standing without leaning, the lead should fall slack. Now move forward.

2 If he bounds ahead, causing the lead to become tight, hold it tightly into your stomach and stand still. (If he runs forward at speed, lean back slightly in anticipation of the jolt as he stops.) Try to anticipate the lead becoming tight. In this way, he will get a sharp tug on the lead when he gets a certain distance from you and will have to stop when he wants to go forward.

3 Make him stand up straight again so the lead goes slack by giving short, sharp tugs. Move forward when the lead is slack. If he runs around or behind you, stand still. Lure him so that he is back in position and begin again.

4 Repeat stage 3 until your dog begins to concentrate on keeping the lead slack. When he is doing so, praise him quietly and tell him how good he is.

Use humane methods

Never use check or choke chains to stop a dog pulling. They can cause discomfort and long-term damage to his neck. Using an ordinary collar and lead is just as effective and more humane.

THE 'SIT'

The 'sit' requires some patience to achieve initially. As your dog begins to work out what is required it will get easier. It may be helpful to back him up against a wall so that he cannot just run backwards as you try to do this. Dogs that have been previously trained by being positioned may also respond to some gentle pressure on their rump. However, if this does not work, revert to using a food lure as illustrated in the method shown here.

Gradually, your dog will begin to understand what is required and will start to sit down as you move the titbit over his head. When this happens, start to give the 'sit' command just before you move your hand towards him so that he can begin to make the association between the word and his action. Practise this over many short sessions.

Practise regularly

Once your dog is automatically sitting as you hold a titbit up to his nose, conceal the titbit in your hand. Eventually you will be able to make the action of approaching his nose with the titbit into a hand signal. Continue to practise, always giving the command just before the hand signal and gradually reducing the hand signal until just the word remains.

1 Use food to lure your dog into the required position. Hold a titbit between thumb and finger just above his nose.

2 He will raise his nose to try to eat the titbit. Move the titbit in such a way that he continues to raise his nose in a backward direction.

3 As his head goes up and back, his bottom should go down into the sit as he tries to balance himself. When it does, feed the titbit and praise him. Keep praising while he stays in position and stop when it is time to get up.

THE 'DOWN'

When your dog has learned to sit at your request, you can move on to teaching the 'down'. Again, you will need a tasty titbit as a lure and a reward. Don't forget to praise him enthusiastically when he responds and does what you want him to do.

1 Use a titbit to lure your dog into position. First, you must get him to sit (see page 108).

2 Bring the titbit down between his front paws. It will take patience at first, but persevere, keeping all hand movements slow and deliberate, and he will soon learn how to respond.

3 If your dog has tried many times to get the titbit and is getting fed up, give him the odd piece of food just for lowering his head to keep him interested. If he stands up, get him back into a sit position and try again.

4 As soon as he begins to lie down, praise him and then feed him the titbit and praise profusely when his elbows touch the ground.

Practise this command

In the same way as for the sit, you should practise this command many times in short sessions. Begin to conceal the food and develop the hand signal, and, finally, phase out the hand signal to leave just the word. Practise in a variety of different places and with him in different positions relative to you.

THE 'STAND'

This is achieved in a similar way to the sit and down, but due to the way in which dogs learn, you should keep in mind that if you teach your dog to stand from the sitting position, he will not understand you if you ask him to stand from the down position. You will need to teach him all over again from the down position if you want him to understand the word properly.

1 From the sit position, lure your dog forwards with a tasty titbit.

If it goes wrong

It does not matter if you make a mistake when using reward-based training. Simply withhold the titbit, make a fuss of your dog and start again.

2 Always try to keep the titbit in line with your dog's nose and just in front of it.

3 Reward him as soon as he is on his feet. If he walks forwards, move your hand more slowly next time and feed the titbit as soon as his back end has come up.

THE 'ROLL OVER'

Only try this exercise once you have mastered the 'down'. Your dog will need to be very relaxed to do this and it is helpful if he is lying on something soft. Practise this until he understands what he needs to do. Eventually you should be able to roll him right over without touching him as he follows your hand round.

1 Begin with your dog in a relaxed down position on a soft surface. Lure his nose round towards his bottom.

Teaching the commands

To get your dog into position, use a food lure to move his head so that his body follows. Getting him into position takes time and patience at first, but once he realizes that he will be rewarded for taking up certain positions, it will be easy to teach him to do so on command.

2 Gradually lure his head over his shoulder. (If it is difficult to get him here, reward him a few times in this position.)

3 Allow him enough time to adjust and then feed him there to reinforce the position.

4 Reward him well as he rolls over and let him know how pleased you are.

THE 'STAY'

Having a dog who will reliably stay in a place where you have put him can be useful on many occasions. It is relatively easy to teach, but it takes time to make your dog reliable in times of excitement. Don't teach the 'stay' until your dog has learnt to take up any position on request. Practise often, gradually building up the time he stays in place until he will stay sitting for five minutes.

1 With your dog in the sit beside you, give a hand signal, e.g. the flat of your hand held in front of his face for a second, and tell him to stay. Stand beside him without moving and praise him for staying put. Anticipate any movement and stop him, using the lead and collar, if he tries to move. If he gets up, replace him, repeat the command and the hand signal and praise him when he stays still. Reward him while he is in position. Release him with a separate command, e.g. 'finish', to end the exercise and ignore him as he moves off. He will learn that he gets rewarded for staying still, but not for moving.

2 When he will stay still while you stand beside him, take one small, slow step away from him. Correct him immediately if he moves, and praise him if he stays still. In this way, gradually build up to moving further away from him over several sessions.

3 When he is happy to sit still while you walk around him, begin to build up the level of distractions that are happening around him. Eventually, you can also practise asking him to stay when he really wants to do something else.

THE 'SETTLE DOWN'

The 'settle down' is a very useful exercise to teach for those times when you do not want your dog to be up and active (such as when you go out visiting or are visited by friends who are afraid of dogs). Begin this exercise after you have taught the 'down'. Practise at a time when you are sitting down and resting.

Attach a lead to your dog's collar and then ask him to lie down. Roll his hips over gently until he is in a relaxed position. Praise him periodically and give him a chew to gnaw on so that he has something to do.

Put the lead under your foot so that he cannot wander off and return him to position if he tries to get up. Keep him there for short periods at first, gradually increasing the time as he learns what is expected of him.

Left: Puppies that learn to settle down can be taken out and about to more places and may have a better life as a result.

AIM FOR SUCCESS

During training, particularly with a young or adolescent dog, do not give commands that cannot be enforced (e.g. do not give him the signal to come if he is off the lead, half a field away and running after a rabbit). Instead, only give commands when you are in a position to get your dog to comply if he does not respond.

Give just one command and ensure that you do something about it if he does not respond. It is probably best to assume that he did not understand and to lure or guide him into the required action so you can then praise him. If you do this every time you ask him to do something, your dog will learn that he has little choice but to comply. If, instead, you give commands that he ignores and do not back them up with action, he will become desensitized to your voice and unresponsive.

Unrewarding behaviour

Actions that are not rewarded are less likely to be repeated. When we attempt to train a dog, we need to ensure that unwanted behaviour or action is not rewarded accidentally. Since some of these actions, such as moving away from a 'stay', are often rewarding in themselves, we need to be one step ahead and prevent them from happening.

GAMES YOU CAN PLAY

Dogs tend to play one of three games: chase games, tug-of-war games and games with squeaky toys. Your dog will have a preference for one type of game. This will be determined mostly by his genetic make-up. For example, collies and other herding dogs prefer chase, bull terriers prefer tug-of-war, and

Left: Many dogs enjoy tugging games. Adults should supervise children and help them to win if necessary.

Jack Russell Terriers prefer games with squeaky toys. If your dog has a favourite game, play it with him. Trying to change the game to one you prefer does not always work and can result in a frustrated dog that prefers not to play with you at all.

Games are an energy outlet

Dogs evolved from a species that needed to hunt to survive. When man first domesticated them, he bred them to do specific jobs and gave them plenty of work to do. Now, pet dogs have no job other than to entertain us. Many loving owners provide everything their dog needs to keep his body healthy but expect him to lie around the house all day while they get on with their busy lives. This may suit some dogs, but not the majority, especially those that were bred to have the mental strength and stamina to work all day.

In the absence of hunting or work to do, dogs need an outlet for all the mental energy they have. Games with toys help to do this, providing an outlet for both physical and mental energy and a way of strengthening the bond between you and your dog. Dogs that are playing with their owners are not getting into trouble with other dogs in the park, chasing livestock or running away from home to find more excitement. Dogs that play with their owners are likely to be more sociable and more in tune with people generally.

MIND GAMES

Try to play with your dog as often as possible. It is better to split up a long play session into several shorter ones that occur periodically throughout the day. In this way, your dog will have something to look forward to and you can use the play sessions as a reward for good behaviour.

Playing outside in the garden or on walks will release more physical energy, but you will need also to invent games that can be played inside during bad weather. Teaching your dog to play 'hide and seek' games with toys, or other games that require you to put in just minimum effort, will make it more likely that you will choose to play them more often.

Playing with toys

All dogs enjoy playing but some don't know how to play with toys and need to be taught. Begin with soft toys, which they will enjoy holding in their mouths, and keep them moving fast and erratically.

Concentrate on the toy rather than your dog and be as exciting and child-like as possible. Encourage any move he makes towards the toy and keep sessions short at first to ensure that he is still interested next time. You may find that putting food inside the toy encourages his interest and makes it more likely that he will try to grab it. Building up the ability to play in this way takes time, but it is well worth it.

Using mental energy

In addition to playing games, by training your dog and teaching him tricks and how to be useful around the house, you will tire him mentally. A dog that lives his life with you, goes out often and accompanies you on excursions will be using up his mental energy and be better behaved. However, a dog that is kept mostly in the kitchen or garden and only taken out occasionally is likely to have too much energy to control and will be very difficult to live with and take out.

Above: Most dogs will enjoy chase and retrieving games, particularly the collies and herding dogs.

TYPES OF GAMES

Different dogs enjoy different types of games. There are two types of interactive games that owners can play with their dogs: tugging and chase games.

Tugging games

These games are enjoyed by dogs from the guarding breeds, Boxers, bull terriers and dogs with a strong, possessive character. It is advisable to win more often than you lose and to take the toy away with you at the end of the game. This will ensure that your dog always thinks you are stronger than him.

LETTING GO OF A TOY

Some adult dogs and puppies can be very reluctant to let go of a toy once they have it in their mouths. It is a good idea to practise taking

Above: Bull terriers love to play tug-of-war but make sure you win more games than you lose.

Right: Teach your puppy to leave a toy on request; offer incentives so it is worth his while to give up his favourite game.

the toy away when the puppy is very small so it will be easier later on when he is bigger and stronger.

Let him hold the toy for a short time while you praise him. Slowly take hold of the toy from underneath where he cannot see your hand. Pull the toy slowly towards you, holding it tightly and keeping it as still as possible. Ask him to 'leave' and produce a small, tasty titbit and wave it under his nose. Be patient and he should let go of the toy to get the titbit. Feed the titbit and throw the toy again for him to chase. In this way, you will soon be able to get him to leave the toy easily. Once he lets go every time you ask, offer the titbits at random as a reward.

Games with toys are a good opportunity to teach your puppy to be careful with his teeth. Every time he bites you, even if it is an accident, take the toy away and end the game. He will soon learn to be more careful and will try to keep his teeth away from your skin.

CHASE GAMES

These are enjoyed by the majority of dogs, especially those from the herding breeds. Let your dog chase the toy; do not chase after him. Teach him to retrieve toys (see page 128) so that he brings them back to you to throw again.

Controlling the chase

If your dog enjoys chase games and is very excited by movement, it is important that you keep control of these desires. If you begin this process while your puppy is still young, it will be easier to control him when he attempts an inappropriate chase later on.

Right: Use soft toys at first to encourage a reluctant puppy to play, moving on to harder toys as he becomes stronger and more skillful.

Left: Encourage your puppy to hold objects in his mouth by praising him whenever he picks something up and carries it.

Above: Chasing a young dog when he has a toy will teach him to stay out of reach, and it will be very difficult to teach him to retrieve later.

A good way to teach him to control his desire to chase is to make him wait while a toy is thrown. Only teach this once he is very keen to chase the toy. Before you throw the toy, ask him to wait and slip a piece of line through his collar. Hold both ends and throw the toy. Make him wait until he calms down and then ask him to 'fetch' and let go of one of the ends of the line so that it slips through his collar. By doing this he will learn to deal with the frustration of not being able to chase whatever he wants and will learn to listen to you rather than to his own desires.

RETRIEVING GAMES

Teaching your dog to retrieve is a useful exercise as it enables you to get the toys back again easily during games. It is also the basis of most other games and many tricks that you can teach your dog. Getting a good basic retrieve helps to put you in control of the games and helps to build the right sort of attitude between you and your dog. It is best to begin while your puppy is still very young and has not yet learned to avoid you when he has something in his mouth.

There are many ways to teach the retrieve and which one is right for you will depend on the age of your dog and his experience. The basic method is given here but before you start, your dog will need to be very interested in playing with toys.

Teaching a puppy

1 Tease him with a soft, lightweight toy that he can easily carry. Try to get him really interested in the toy.

2 Throw it a small distance away and encourage him to run forward and pick it up. If he does not pick it up, flick it away from him so that the movement entices him to grab and hold it. When your puppy is holding it, encourage him to come to you. If necessary, run backwards to encourage him to follow.

3 As he comes to you, keep your hands away from his head and neck as this may cause him to avoid you in an effort to keep his toy. Praise and stroke him to encourage him to stay with you. After a few moments, take the toy away, then throw it for him to chase. He will learn that giving you the toy is a good idea as it leads to another game.

Teaching an adult dog

1 Choose a quiet, familiar place, such as the back garden, and choose a time when your dog is ready to play. Attach a long piece of thin line to his collar to trail along the ground behind him (for this reason, you should not use a flexi-lead).

2 Produce his favourite toy, wave it in front of him and tease him with it for a few moments. When he becomes excited, throw the toy so that it moves fast and lands not too far away. Encourage him to pick it up, saying 'fetch' excitedly.

3 When he has the toy, do not move towards him. Pick up the end of the line attached to his collar and call him to you. If he does not come, encourage him  with gentle tugs on the line, running backwards. Praise him enthusiastically as he comes closer.

4 Praise him quietly and stroke his back when he is close enough to do so. Do not grab the toy as this will make him want to avoid you in the future so that he can keep it.

5 After a few moments, take it and repeat the retrieve. If he resists, try holding the toy firmly with one hand and placing a tasty titbit in front of his nose. Give a signal, e.g. 'leave', so you can eventually get him to let go on command.

Find a toy

This game involves your dog learning to find an object that is not on view and is hidden somewhere in the house or garden. Once he knows the game it can provide him with hours of fun and activity while you sit down and rest!

Begin by holding on to your dog's collar and showing him a favourite toy. Throw it so that it lands out of sight, e.g. behind a sofa or in long grass. Wait for a few moments before you release him to find it. Ask him to 'find' as he goes out to search for it. After a few repetitions, walk him away from the place from which

Above: Finding a toy in long grass will be fun for your dog and uses up lots of energy.

Above: Teaching your puppy to find toys hidden somewhere in the house uses up lots of his energy without tiring you.

you threw the toy and turn him around a few times before releasing him to find it. Praise and make a big fuss of him when he finds it. Once he is happy to find an article that he has seen thrown, gradually progress to asking him to find one that you have placed in advance. Indicate the area you want him to search and place two or three large items in that area at first to ensure he is successful.

MAKE THE GAME MORE FUN
Practise this until he will go and search for items whenever you ask him to 'find'. Slowly progress until he will search the house or garden for named items, some of which may contain food for added interest.

Playing messenger

This enjoyable game for all the family involves teaching the dog to 'go to' a named person in order to receive a reward. Messages can then be tucked into the dog's collar or you can teach him to carry a container that carries the message to that person. It can be fun to play this game with children and dogs.

THE NEXT STAGE

When your dog has mastered this trick (opposite), try doing it with the other person in the next room. Ensure that the other person praises your dog enthusiastically and produces a titbit when he arrives. Practise until you can send your dog to find that person anywhere in the house and also until he can 'go to' all the people who live in the house. Repeat stages 1 and 2 using a different person. Next you can teach your dog to carry objects to the named person, or tuck messages in his collar to make it fun for humans, too.

Left: This puppy is being taught to play messenger. This is an enjoyable way for your puppy to interact with everyone in the family.

1 Get your dog to sit beside you. Ask him to 'go to' a named person who is sitting in the same room as you get up and move towards that person.

2 As your dog approaches that person, they should produce a titbit and lure him closer, feeding the titbit as he gets there. Repeat this many times over several sessions until he runs over to that person as soon as you give the command.

Fetch and carry

Once your dog has mastered the basic retrieve, and will happily go and fetch any toy you point out to him, it is time to begin to teach him to fetch items other than his toys. When introducing a new item, make it into a retrieving game. You want your dog to enjoy picking up the article so keep it fun. Begin with soft items that are easy to carry, working up to harder objects which are more difficult. Many dogs are put off by the feel of a brush's bristles or metal, so leave such objects until last. Progress until your dog will go and fetch anything to which you point. Once he will pick up just about anything you ask for, the next step is to teach him to carry things for you.

Ask your dog to fetch an article and, as he brings it, begin to walk away. Keep encouraging him to come with you and turn around so that he is walking beside you. After a few paces, praise and reward him well. If he drops the article, encourage him to fetch it again.

Left: Teaching your dog to fetch and carry objects enables him to help you around the house and will make his life more interesting too.

FETCH MY SLIPPERS

If you would like your dog to learn to fetch named objects, such as slippers or newspapers, begin by offering him the choice between two toys. Put them out in front of him and ask him to fetch the toy that he is most likely to pick up. If he brings back the wrong toy, take it quietly and ask him again to 'fetch the ...'. As soon as he picks up the right toy, show him how pleased you are. Keep practising, over several sessions, until he will retrieve the named toy from a group of other toys. Then move on to teaching him the names of other objects you want him to bring back in a similar way.

Below: Fetching slippers is useful and gives your dog a job to do. Remember to reward him well.

OTHER GAMES

There are three types of games we can set up for our dogs to play by themselves: searching games, digging games and games with squeaky toys.

Games with squeaky toys

These are enjoyed by terriers and other dogs with a strong predatory instinct. How determined your dog is to kill the squeak will give you an indication of how strong his predatory nature is. Dogs that like squeaky toy games will often enjoy catching and killing small animals. For dogs that are very excited by this game, you may have to replace the squeak frequently.

Right: Terriers usually enjoy games with squeaky toys as they simulate the noise made by captured prey.

Above: Providing a special digging area can help to prevent your dog digging in flower beds or the lawn.

Digging games

These are enjoyed by terriers or dogs from breeds bred to go to ground, such as the Dachshund. Create a visually marked area to be used as a digging pit and teach your dog to find buried bones and chews there.

Searching games

These games are enjoyed by all dogs once they have learned how to play. You can teach your dog how to find hidden objects by rolling toys into long grass and then releasing them with a 'find' command. Develop this game over time until your dog can find a hidden object in any area.

COPING WITH PLAY-BITING

While still in the litter, puppies will play together by grabbing each other with their mouths and holding on. When your new puppy comes into your home, he will try to do the same to you.

How to stop play-biting

The natural reaction for most owners is to tell their dog off, but this will be confusing for him since he meant no harm, intending only to invite them to play. For this reason, it is better to teach him an alternative way to play with you. Have a toy ready to offer him, preferably a soft toy for very young puppies as this will be more acceptable than hard rubber toys.

If your puppy chooses your hand instead of the toy, make a fist and keep it very still. With the other hand, move the toy fast and erratically so that it becomes more enticing. Praise him whenever he begins to bite on the toy instead of you. Keep the game interesting by keeping the toy moving so that he does not become bored and try to bite you again.

At first, and for some time, he will try to get you to play in the way that worked while he was still in the litter. However, gradually, he will learn how to play acceptably and the mouthing will begin to subside.

CRY OUT

Another method for stopping persistent biting at a time when you do not have a toy close by is to cry out loudly as if in pain whenever he sinks his teeth into you. (This may not be so difficult to do as it is likely that he will hurt when he bites!) This will probably make him wag his tail and try to lick you, but do not get into a situation where you shriek, he gets excited and bites harder, and you shriek more.

1 Make a fist with the hand your puppy tries to bite and keep it still. Shake the toy vigorously with the other hand.

2 Praise him when he begins to bite the toy instead and have an exciting game with him.

TEACHING TRICKS

Tricks are easy to teach and can be fun for spectators and the dog. Never teach anything that is demeaning or undignified. Tricks should show how clever your dog is and how nice it is to have a dog that is well trained.

Nor should you teach anything that is hazardous. For instance, do not teach puppies to jump until they are mature as it can injure growing bones and joints. Keep lessons short and fun and always end on success.

Tricks that are easiest to teach are those that involve natural traits. For example, terriers enjoy using their paws and are easy to teach tricks that involve pawing at something. Retrievers and other gun dogs like to use their mouths and are good at learning tricks that involve holding objects. Energetic, agile dogs enjoy tricks that involve running or jumping.

Be inventive

Like children, dogs get bored with doing things routinely. To get the best from your dog, be inventive about games, vary the tasks you set him and change the rewards every so often. If you do this, he will stay interested and willing to please, and you will have more fun, too.

TEACHING SIMPLE TRICKS

If you have mastered the basic exercises, teaching your dog tricks should be quite easy. Choose simple tricks at first and work up gradually to those that are more difficult. Always break up complicated tricks into stages and teach the last stage first. In this way, when you begin to teach an earlier stage, your dog will be moving towards a part of the trick that he knows and finds easy.

1 Support the paw lightly rather than hold on which may make him withdraw it.

2 Reward the desired behaviour immediately with a tasty treat.

High five!

Asking a puppy or an adult dog to wave or do a 'high five' is a very easy trick to teach.

1 With your puppy sitting in front of you, tickle the hairs behind one of his front paws gently until he lifts his foot. As he does so, ask him to give a paw and praise him well. Lift the foot up gently on the flat of your hand and feed a treat. Progress until he will raise his paw on command.

2 Gradually ask him to raise his paw higher before rewarding him. You can then develop a 'wave' or bring your hand in to touch his paw in a 'high five'.

Which one?

This trick involves teaching your dog to use his nose to find out which flower pot a treat (or toy) is hidden under and to indicate which one it is by placing his paw on top. It is a complicated trick so you will need to break it down into stages.

1 Begin first by teaching your dog to put his paw on top of a flowerpot to receive a treat.
2 Now get him to decide between two pots, one of which has the food hidden underneath. You can shuffle the pots to make it more fun. When your dog paws the right pot he gets the treat.
3 Gradually work up to more pots.

Below: 'Tell me which one'. By using his sensitive nose, this dog detects which pot the toy is under. He indicates this to his owner by touching it with a paw.

Other ideas for tricks

You can be as inventive as you like when teaching tricks, or you can choose one from this list.

SSHH!
The dog is quiet on command.

PRESS HERE FOR ACTION!
The dog presses a pedal to get a treat.

DANCE WITH ME
The dog weaves in and out of your legs as you walk.

FIND THE QUEEN
The dog paws at the appropriate playing card.

OVER!
The dog jumps a small jump.

Left: Jumping is fun for dogs but do not attempt to teach them this until they have matured and their bones and joints are no longer soft.

Right: Agility is fun for dogs and helps to keep them fit.

SPEAK!
The dog barks on command.

HOOPS
The dog jumps through a hoop.

IT'S COLD IN HERE
The dog shuts the door.

ATTICHOO!
The dog pulls a handkerchief out of a pocket and passes it to his owner.

Right: This puppy can take the handkerchief out of his owner's pocket and give it to him whenever he sneezes.

CURING COMMON PROBLEMS

Many behaviour problems will improve or even disappear altogether if the relationship between the owner and dog is improved, if all the essential needs of the dog are met and if training is carried out correctly. There is not space here to go into all the behaviour problems and their solutions adequately but some advice has been given as a starting point.

Always try not to resort to punishment. Behaviour can be very frustrating for owners and there is a great temptation to resort to threats and violence to get a result. However, punishment rarely works and can harm the relationship between you, resulting in further problems. If your dog often engages in an unwanted behaviour, then try to think through a possible solution that does not involve punishment. If you are unable to do so, seek further help from a good pet behaviour counsellor.

Left: If you do not provide your puppy with a constant supply of suitable items to chew, he will resort to taking things he should not.

BAD MANNERS AND UNRULY BEHAVIOUR

Teach good manners in the same way as you teach other exercises. Show your dog what you want him to do, praise and reward him for good behaviour and teach him a command for the required action. Since much unwanted behaviour is self-rewarding, you must find a way to prevent it while you teach him how rewarding the appropriate behaviour can be.

Use physical control to stop him being rewarded by the unwanted behaviour. Use gentle restraint, via a collar and lead, or remove whatever is causing the inappropriate behaviour from temptation temporarily. You can then manipulate him into showing the correct behaviour which you can reward. He will soon get into the habit of behaving as you want him to.

Right: Do not allow a puppy to be too rough. It can become a bad habit which can be difficult to stop later.

PREVENTING AGGRESSION

In the wild, competing over food and items of interest is a useful strategy to ensure that you get enough to eat. In our world, there is no need to compete in this way and it is important to teach this to your dog.

Puppies will grow up into nervous adults if they are undersocialized or have enough bad experiences to make them fearful. Nervous adults are likely to bite if they feel that defence is their only option for avoiding a dangerous or painful experience. Sensitive, alert, reactive types of dog are more likely to be fearful and, hence, to turn into dogs that bite unless special care is taken to avoid this happening. If you are starting out with a puppy, it is quite easy to ensure that he becomes a confident, friendly dog that uses defensive behaviour as an absolute last resort.

Left: Watch for signs that your puppy is anxious and take action to make the situation more pleasant for him.

Above: Puppies that meet and have fun with lots of people from an early age will be less apprehensive and less likely to bite defensively when they are older.

Socialize well

Socialize your puppy with people, including children, and other animals from an early age. This will ensure that he feels comfortable with the different things that people do and does not feel apprehensive when they grab him or do unusual things to him. A well-socialized dog will accept strange behaviour from people and will take unusual occurrences in his stride and is less likely to be afraid.

Don't punish

Dogs that are punished by their owners often view people as slightly unpredictable. Many punishments are administered to dogs for breaking rules they did not know about. All they learn from these punishments is that their owner sometimes becomes aggressive for no good reason. If, on top of this, the owner does not develop a good relationship with their pet, it is

Above: Use positive training methods that will reward your puppy for doing the right thing rather than punishing his bad behaviour.

Above. Rather than punishing natural behaviours like digging, provide an alternative outlet for the drive, such as a digging pit.

likely that the dog will view humans with mistrust. This leads to fear and defensive aggression when people do unusual things and can result in an unexpected bite during normal interactions with people.

To avoid this, do not resort to punishment to get your own way. Try to win encounters without the use of force, train your puppy using positive methods, and teach him what you want him to do and praise and reward him for doing so.

Avoid nasty experiences

While your puppy is growing up, protect him from anything frightening or unpleasant. Experiences that cause pain or fright can make a lasting impression and are likely to cause dogs to become fearful when they find themselves in a similar situation later on.

FOOD

All dogs should be taught that hands come to give, not take. To do this, give your dog his dinner but withhold the tasty portion if you feed fresh meat, or collect some smelly, tasty treats if you feed a complete food. Allow him to eat a few mouthfuls and then approach offering something much nicer than he has in his bowl. Do this on several occasions throughout his meal. Gradually, over several days, get closer to his bowl with your hand before allowing him to take the food. Eventually, he should welcome your hands being placed near his bowl as he learns that they will deliver something tasty.

Left: Rawhide chews need to be replaced quite often but they are an ideal way for a puppy to exercise his jaws.

CHEWS AND BONES

Get your dog accustomed to being approached when
he has chews or bones. Begin with chews that are less
palatable and work up to bones. When he has been
chewing for some time, lure him away with a smelly,
tasty titbit, taking the chew with the other hand. After
he has eaten the titbit, give him back the chew.

TOYS

If your dog is aggressive over possessions, teach him to
retrieve (see page 128). Do not chase him and become
aggressive. This will make him more likely to bite. If he
runs off with things, attach a line to his collar in the house.

Above: Dogs need to learn not to be possessive of things
that are imporant to them such as food and toys.

Aggression towards other dogs

For solutions to problems of aggression towards other dogs, you would be well advised to find a good pet behaviour counsellor to help you. If, however, your dog only barks and gets excited if he sees another dog, it may be possible to focus his attention on to you instead. Most dogs bark and lunge forward because they are fearful of other dogs and have learnt that behaving in this way keeps the other dog away from them. In addition, their owner often pulls them back so the distance between them and the dog they are scared of increases which reduces the threat.

Below: Teaching your puppy that you are the most exciting thing in the world rather than other dogs can prevent many problems later in adulthood.

Some dogs that show this behaviour are fine when off the lead as they can run away or avoid other dogs. It is often only when they are tethered to their owner and cannot get away that they learn to behave badly.

With the advent of puppy socialization classes, there are an increasing number of dogs that have learnt to enjoy playing with other dogs and are desperate to get to them when they see them while out on a walk. Dogs that have been allowed to play many games with other dogs to the exclusion of games

Above: Well-socialized dogs enjoy meeting others, but not all dogs will welcome their attentions.

with their owners will often become very frustrated when their freedom is restricted by a lead. This frustration can cause aggressive behaviour and it is often hard to tell the difference between this behaviour and that caused by fear.

FOCUSING ATTENTION ON YOU

If you are experiencing problems of barking or excitement when your dog sees another (if it is severe, get professional help), you should be able to improve his behaviour by refocusing him on to you. Find an open space where dogs are playing in the distance. Allow him to settle and then invite him to play or to take titbits from you.

Use whatever motivates him most and praise him and reward him well for concentrating on you for a short time. If he would rather focus on the other dogs, wait until he has got bored with watching them and try again. (If he is taking a long time to stop looking at them, put more distance between you and them.)

NO ROUGH AND TUMBLE

It is not a good idea to encourage a young puppy to play rough-and-tumble games with humans unless you are an experienced dog owner, particularly if your puppy will grow into a large dog. These games usually encourage a dog to bite human hands and

Above: Rough and tumble games with littermates are essential for learning how to play with other dogs but should be discouraged once your puppy comes to live with humans.

arms and to use their strength against you. Dogs that have learned how to bite humans will be much more practised if they need to do so in defence later and so these games are best avoided.

It is very important that children do not play in this way since a puppy will usually learn he is stronger, faster and better at being in control as he grows up. It is better that children learn to play games with toys with their puppy so that they can stay in control.

PREVENTING NOISY BARKING

Barking is a normal behaviour for dogs but it can quickly become a problem if it happens often and for too long. It is most important to find the cause of the problem if you are to prevent the behaviour.

- Dogs often bark to warn the rest of the pack of an intruder.
- Dogs may have learnt to bark when they want their owners' attention.

Barking at an early age

Puppies usually begin to bark when they are between about six and eight months old. They may bark occasionally before this but a well socialized puppy should not begin to bark properly until he is more mature. Some breeds are more vocal than others. German Shepherd Dogs, some terriers and smaller breeds may be excessively vocal from an early age. You must stop this as any habits formed during puppyhood will be very difficult to break later on.

Don't encourage your puppy to bark. Owners who do this because they want a dog that will look after the house find they own a dog that barks excessively at the slightest noise. A well-socialized dog will bark naturally if he hears something suspicious on his territory; there is no need to help him to learn this.

Right: Teaching your dog to 'speak' and 'be quiet' on command will help him to understand what you mean when you ask him to stop barking.

Solving the problem

It is acceptable behaviour for dogs to bark to warn the rest of the pack of an intruder, providing it is not sustained. A distraction, in the form of a game or titbits, will teach your dog to run to you at such times. It is a good way of taking his mind off whatever he is worried about and fixing it onto the reward.

If your dog barks when he wants attention, saying anything to him, even if you are cross with him, will make him more likely to bark next time. The only way to stop it is to make a rule that you will not look at him, speak to him or touch him, ever again, when he is barking. It can take time to achieve, and will get worse before it gets better, but it will work in the end.

PREVENTING CHASING

Dogs that chase things that they should not are usually either having fun or are trying to chase the things away. For dogs that enjoy chasing, particularly those from the herding breeds, their enjoyment needs to be channelled into acceptable games with toys. Dogs that are trying to chase things away because they are worried about them need to learn that those things are not dangerous.

It is not surprising that many dogs from the herding breeds develop problems associated with chase

Above: Unless herding dogs are given work, even chasing a ball, they will find less acceptable outlets for their abilities.

Below: Hounds are often disinterested in playing with toys and prefer to chase animals or people if they can.

behaviour. In the absence of the real thing and any real work to do, they often turn their attentions to cars, bikes, joggers, cats and even shadows.

Play with your dog

If you choose a dog with this genetic make-up, it is essential that you teach him from an early age to play successfully with toys so that you can give him a 'job' to keep him occupied. You should set aside enough time every day to use up the mental and physical energy that he will have as he grows older.

Fortunately, as we select more for dogs who look good, but who do not need to work, many strains or lines are losing such a strong desire to chase, but it will take some time before these susceptible breeds all have good pet dog traits instead.

PREVENTING SEPARATION PROBLEMS

Dogs can be destructive, noisy or dirty when left alone unless they are used to isolation. If your dog chews the furniture or doors, barks, howls or messes when left alone, you will need to find out the cause before you can solve the problem. There are many causes of separation problems but they fall into three distinct categories:

• Boredom/adolescent exploration
• Fear-based problems/insecurity
• Over-attachment

Boredom

Bored dogs chew or bark at the slightest disturbance just for something to do. Adolescent dogs between six and twelve months often chew as they explore their environment. The secret to solving these problems is to tire them out, both physically and mentally, before you leave. A tired

Left: Puppies can get into all sorts of mischief when left alone. Ensure that they are not left with items that they can damage, or which could harm them.

dog is usually asleep rather than engaging in unwanted behaviour. In addition, leave tasty chews and interesting, safe objects to investigate when you are not there.

Left: A Kong stuffed with biscuits or other appetizing items can keep a puppy occupied for a long time.

Right: A cube or ball filled with titbits provides interest for a dog with an active mind and can help to prevent problems caused by boredom when he is left alone.

Leave something to chew

Always ensure that your puppy has enough suitable items to chew when he is left alone (see page 57). If he refuses food or chews when left, it is probably because he is too worried. If this is the case, you will need to work harder to get him used to being left alone.

Anxiety when left

Dogs who are frightened of something can often cope with the fear while you are present to protect them, but become anxious when you leave. Dogs who are fearful often chew something that carries their owner's scent, try to dig a den into a mattress, chair or under a table, and may defecate or urinate in fright as they begin to panic. These dogs need to be desensitized to whatever is frightening them. Leaving articles of clothing that smell of you in strategic places, and making a den-like area in a dark, safe place can also be of temporary help.

Above: Puppies need to be taught to be alone, especially those that live in families where they are rarely left on their own.

Above: Leave something suitable to chew when you leave your puppy alone. If you do not do this, or leave him for too long, you can expect to come back to unwanted damage.

Over-attachment

Dogs who are very attached to their owner or who are not accustomed to being left alone may make frantic attempts to get out of the house when left behind, damaging doors and frames in the process, or may bark and howl to attract their owner's attention. Such dogs need to be taught to accept being left by leaving them for gradually increasing periods of time, beginning with a very short time initially.

PREVENTING FEARFULNESS

Dogs are often scared of things that are unfamiliar, especially if those things move and make loud noises. This trait helps to keep them safe in the wild and it has been handed down, via the genetic code, to our pet dogs today. Consequently, dogs are often afraid of strangers, other dogs, children, things on wheels or noises. This will be particularly true if your dog was not socialized well as a puppy. Dogs like this will spend a lot of their time being anxious and worried when taken into the outside world or when strangers come to visit their home.

Bad experiences

Dogs may become fearful of certain people, animals or experiences because they have been frightened or hurt by them in the past. Consequently, they are often fearful of other dogs, strangers or even owners who may have been aggressive. It only takes one or two unpleasant encounters for the fear to take root and, if it continues over time, it can become generalized until the dog becomes afraid of all other dogs or people.

Often, if the dog is sensitive and the thing causing the fear is something ordinary, such as a person or another dog, an owner will have no idea that their puppy has been scared by such experiences since they are unable to read the body language (see page 42). It is only later on, as the puppy becomes more confident, at about eight months old, that the problem is noticed. At this time, some aggression may be seen, even if it is only in the form of barking and growling in an attempt to keep the thing that scares them away.

Solving the problem

Whatever the reason for the fear, it is important not to force your dog to encounter something of which he is afraid. If you do, he is likely to learn to be aggressive to either keep the thing he is frightened of away, or to prevent you from continuing to scare him.

Right: Shy dogs need to be able to take things at their own pace so they can overcome their fears gradually.

If your dog growls, barks or snaps, he is not happy with the situation. He cannot tell you in any other way, so do not punish him. Try to appreciate that there is little else he can do to get himself out of what he sees as a potentially dangerous situation. Remove him from whatever it is that is upsetting him.

BE A GOOD PACK LEADER

A good pack leader should protect his pack and if your dog sees you taking action in this way he is more likely to rely on you next time rather than deal with the problem himself. It will be up to you to read his body language and anticipate what might scare him.

Punishing him for growling may well stop him from doing so again, but you will not have made him less fearful. Instead, you will have removed his only means of communication that he is upset and he may bite without warning when the fear becomes too great.

OVERCOME HIS FEAR

If your dog is afraid of something, you can overcome his fear gradually by arranging for him to encounter whatever it is in a mild form first. This means putting distance between him and the thing he fears. Use games or titbits to encourage him to have a happy time and be light-hearted yourself. When he can cope at a distance, gradually, over a number of sessions, move closer. Never go faster than he can cope with and go back a stage if he shows distress. Getting him to play with toys or concentrate on tasty titbits can help take his mind off the problem and change his attitude.

GO SLOWLY

Do not expect too much progress too soon. It takes a long time to overcome fears and replace them with a relaxed attitude. Go slowly, letting your dog take things at a pace he can cope with, and you should, gradually, begin to see an improvement in his behaviour.

Above: A young Jack Russell puppy approaches slowly. It is cautious and reserved but unafraid.

PREVENTING ATTENTION SEEKING

Some owners spend more time with their dogs and this encourages a closer bond. Such dogs tend to be the centre of their owner's attention most of the time and it can come as quite a surprise to them when, for example, visitors arrive or the owner answers the telephone, and they find themselves temporarily dismissed. A whole range of unwanted behaviour, such as barking, chewing and biting or scratching the owner, may then be displayed by the dog to try to return things to normal.

Solving the problem

If you usually devote a lot of attention to your puppy or adult dog, you will need to make sure that this sort of attention seeking behaviour does not happen. In order to achieve this, you should give your dog regular periods of 'time out'. This means setting aside at

Right: Try not to give your dog any attention when you have settled down to do something else.

least half an hour daily when you are in the same room as him but, during this time, you should not look at, talk to, touch or speak to him.

If he begins to do something you do not want him to do, physically prevent him but with as little contact as possible. Do not allow him to sit on you or lie down touching you at these times. Stand up and move away instead. In this way, he will learn to cope without you at times when you are busy with more important things.

BE ALOOF

Not responding to all requests from your dog for affection or attention, as well as beginning and ending social interactions to suit you, will raise your status in your dog's eyes and confirm your position as leader of the pack.

Right: Giving periods of 'time out' will result in a dog that is content to leave you in peace sometimes rather than one that will constantly demand your attention.

PREVENTING JUMPING UP

If your dog jumps up when greeting you, he is doing so because he wants to get closer to your face. If you crouch down when greeting him, it will enable him to get closer to you and reduce the need to jump up.

Visitors and strangers

If your dog jumps up or is badly behaved with visitors, look at how he greets you and behaves with you. If you get good manners from him when he is alone with you, he is much more likely to behave well when strangers are present.

Boisterous dogs

If your dog is boisterous and out of control, teach him some exercises to give you some control. Look also at the amount of exercise he is getting since an under-exercised

Right: Jumping up is an annoying habit that is easily controlled by using the right approach.

dog is often boisterous and difficult to live with. It may also be a good idea to check your hierarchy rules as difficult dogs may be too high in status and may need to be brought down to a lower level.

Solving the problem

You can hold on to your dog's collar to prevent him jumping up and tell him to 'sit' instead; he must already know the meaning of 'sit' if this is to work (see page 108). Once he understands that as soon as he sits, you will crouch down and give him your undivided attention, he will be happy to comply with your request. Since jumping up is self-rewarding, ignoring the behaviour will only work if you can successfully turn your back on him and avoid touching, speaking and looking at him until his four feet are on the ground.

Right: Bend down to greet your puppy to help him to realize there is no need to jump up. Rewarding him when all four feet are on the ground makes it more likely that he will wait for you to come down to him next time.

HOUSE TRAINING

Nest animals have an instinctive desire to be clean and will go to the toilet outside their nest as soon as they are able. You can build on this by teaching your puppy that the whole of the house is his nest and that when he wants to go to the toilet he needs to go out into the garden.

If you have obtained your puppy from a breeder who provided a nest and an easily accessible

Above: These puppies will instinctively leave the nest to be clean. This is encouraged by easy access and making a clear distinction between their clean bedding and the newspaper.

toileting/play area, and kept this area clean, you should find it quite easy. If your puppy came from dirty or cramped conditions where there was no distinction between the nest and play areas, you will find it more difficult.

Different puppies learn to be clean at different rates. Gentle, easy-going puppies seem to learn more slowly than confident, strong-willed ones. A new puppy is a very young animal and it will take time for him to learn what to do and to develop enough bodily control to enable him to accomplish what is required. The more time and attention you can give him, the quicker the house-training process will be.

Avoiding accidents indoors

You will need to be aware of what is happening with your puppy at all times so that you do not allow him to make too many mistakes indoors. To prevent him from eliminating indoors, you will need to take him outside at the following times:

- First thing in the morning (immediately, not after, you have put the kettle on!)
- After he has eaten
- When he wakes up from a nap
- After play
- After any excitement (e.g. a member of the family returning home)

Right: Always go outside with your puppy when he needs to go to the toilet. Otherwise he will try to get back inside with you and will probably go on the carpet once you have let him in.

EVERY TWO HOURS

It is not enough to just put your puppy outside by himself. If you do this, he will try to get back inside with you and will not relax enough. You need to go out with him even if it is cold and wet, and wait until he goes to the toilet. Activity and sniffing both seem to stimulate a puppy to go. When he begins, praise him quietly. When he has finished, offer a small, tasty titbit and praise him enthusiastically.

THE TELLTALE SIGNS

If you follow this practice, there should be no need for your puppy to make a mistake indoors. However, life cannot always revolve around a puppy and the odd accident is bound to happen. If you see your puppy showing signs of wanting to go in the house, i.e. sniffing the ground, circling, squatting, run to the door and call him, encouraging him to follow you out of the house. If he has already started, shout loudly enough to stop him and, again, run to the door, and encourage him to follow. Go out with him and follow the usual procedure. Clean up any soiled areas with a solution of biological washing powder to remove the smell that may attract him back to the same spot.

USE A PLAYPEN

At night, when you have to go out or when you cannot concentrate on your puppy, confine him to a playpen with a nest area and a large area covered with newspaper so he can go on this if he needs to.

WATCH FOR THE SIGNS

Gradually, your puppy will begin to prefer to go outside rather than in the house and he will try to wait until this is possible. Watch for any small signs that he needs to go, such as running to the back door, and reward him immediately by going into the garden with him. It takes time for some puppies to be able to last out all night, so don't expect too much until he is at least six months.

Right: Sniffing seems to speed up the process of going to the toilet and is necessary for selecting the right spot to go.

PREVENTING CAR TRAVEL PROBLEMS

Solving car travel probolems depends upon finding the cause. Owners will often attempt to punish dogs that bark in the car. This rarely works as they are trying to treat the symptoms rather than looking at the underlying cause. Without removing the motivation for the behaviour, the dog will continue to do what he wants to do and it will be very difficult to stop him.

Excitable dogs

Dogs can behave badly in the car because they are excited at the prospect of a walk and this is the only time they travel by car. The association between the car and the walk is soon made and the dog begins barking with excitement in anticipation of getting out and having fun. A good game in the garden will tire your dog out before putting him in the car. Taking him on journeys that do not end in a walk will help.

Wait for at least five minutes at the end of any car journey or until he is calm and settled so that the car ride is associated with a boring wait when the car stops instead of wild activity. Take a magazine to read while you wait, and when you get out, keep your dog on the lead for a while and do some quiet lead exercises before letting him loose.

Above: If the early journeys in the car are pleasant and not frightening, your puppy will soon accept car travel as part of life. Don't just use the car to take him to the vet!

Nervous dogs

Dogs may behave badly in the car because they are afraid of the movement. They will be happy to sit in a stationary car but will become agitated when it moves. Some may be sick, while others will jump around and bark to relieve their anxiety. They will often settle on long journeys on straight roads but will get anxious again when the car begins to turn corners.

These dogs will need to be desensitized gradually to being in the car and to its movement. In extreme cases, you may have to get them over their fear of getting into the car. Use toys and food to speed up the process. Get them feeling happy about sitting in a stationary car, then take them on very short journeys at first (maybe a few hundred metres) and gradually build up to longer distances. Always end the journey with something enjoyable, such as a walk or dinner.

Dogs that chase

Dogs that enjoy chasing often become wildly excited in the car because they see things moving past them at speed. They will often focus on something that is approaching, such as a tree or a person, and then spin round as it goes past. Since the dog is prevented from

chasing the object, he often barks in frustration or may even resort to tearing chunks out of the upholstery. Dogs that do this need to be

Left: Dogs that behave well in the car are more likely to be taken out more often.

Above: The foot-well in the front of a car can help dogs feel more relaxed. You may need to tether your dog at first to ensure he cannot move over to you and interfere with your driving.

confined in such a way that prevents them from seeing out of the windows. Teach them to lie down in the foot well of the passenger seat or use a travelling crate which is partially covered so they cannot see out.

Barking in the car

Dogs that bark at their owners while they are driving because they want attention often do this at home too. If your dog barks in the car while looking directly at you and also demands your attention at home, you will need to change his behaviour in the house first before tackling the problem in the car.

PREVENTING VET'S VISIT PROBLEMS

Many dogs are afraid of being examined by a veterinary surgeon and some will try to bite and may have to be muzzled. You will often see dogs in the waiting room at your vet's surgery shaking, drooling and whining with anxiety. There may be many reasons why some dogs are afraid of going to the vet, but the problem often begins during puppyhood.

Problems start in puppyhood

Most puppies visit the veterinary surgery two or three times for vaccinations. The injections should not hurt, but the experience of going somewhere new, meeting

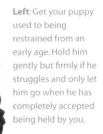

Left: Get your puppy used to being restrained from an early age. Hold him gently but firmly if he struggles and only let him go when he has completely accepted being held by you.

Right: When lifting your puppy, make sure that you support his weight with a hand underneath his bottom. If he feels secure, he will be less likely to struggle.

other dogs in the waiting room, then being put on a table and handled by a stranger may be overwhelming for a puppy that isn't prepared for it. If this happens and later, when the puppy is older, an uncomfortable procedure or examination is done, a fear of the vet is put in place which is difficult to eradicate later on.

PREVENTING PROBLEMS

Accustom him early on to all the things that you or your veterinary surgeon may want to do to him at a later date. For instance, you should teach him to accept nail clipping, teeth inspection and cleaning, grooming and bathing.

Right: Look in the ears while holding the head still and practise wiping the outer edges with a tissue. Exercises like this make life much easier should you ever need to give your dog medication for an ear condition.

Below: Lift the lips to expose the teeth and check his mouth. Try not to cover the eyes and ears or he may struggle. Once he has accepted this, gently open the mouth. Let go quickly and reward him. Gradually build up until you can hold the jaws open for longer.

GOOD SOCIALIZATION

Your puppy should be well socialized by the breeder so that at the time of his first vaccination he is happy to meet and be handled by strangers. You should take him out and about so that he gets used to meeting other animals and being in new situations. If you develop a good relationship with him, he will view humans as trustworthy and he will also look to you to protect him in times of uncertainty.

If your puppy is still shy, ask if you can take him back to socialize with the nurses and to practise having him examined when more time is available. A good veterinary practice will welcome this as they know that puppies who have had good experiences early on make easier, more friendly patients when they become adults.

Right: Encounters like this can be very frightening for your puppy if he is shy and he is having too many new experiences at once. Make sure that he has many similar encounters that are pleasant soon afterwards or he may be worried about visiting the vet.

USEFUL INFORMATION

Training classes will help you to learn the skills and techniques needed to train your dog effectively, and provide valuable help and encouragement. Classes vary in quality so select carefully from those available. Only go to those that use reward-based methods in a friendly, easy-to-learn environment. Avoid those where check chains or force is used and where the mood is humiliating or chaotic.

If your dog has a behaviour problem, you will need to find someone who has an in-depth understanding of dog behaviour. They need to have been working with dogs for many years in order to gain the necessary experience, so check their work history carefully. A recommendation from someone who has tried out their methods or a referral from a vet is often the best way to find the right person. Also, they should be using only effective, humane methods so be sure to avoid anyone who offers quick fixes in the form of aversion or punishment.

Useful addresses

PUPPY SCHOOL
PO Box 186
Chipping Norton
Oxon OX7 3XG
www.puppyschool.co.uk

**ASSOCIATION OF
PET DOG TRAINERS**
Peacocks Farm
Northchapel
Petworth
West Sussex GU28 9JB

**ASSOCIATION OF PET
BEHAVIOUR COUNSELLORS**
P.O. Box 46
Worcester WR8 9YS
Tel: 01386 751151
email: apbc@petbcent.demon.co.uk
http://webzone1.co.uk/www/apbc.org.uk

THE BLUE CROSS
Shilton Road, Burford, Oxon OX18 4PF
Tel: 01993 822651

INDEX

If you have enjoyed this book, why not learn more about 'man's best friend' with other Collins titles?

A superbly illustrated guide to the fascinating world of dog showing

128pp £14.99

HB   0 00 713468 1

Expert advice on choosing and living with over 130 breeds of dogs

256pp £4.99

PB   0 00 717802 6

The Collins Dog Owner's Guides series includes:

Boxer **0 00 413370 6**, Cocker Spaniel **0 00 717607 4**,
English Springer Spaniel **0 00 717605 8**, German Shepherd **0 00 717833 6**,
Labrador **0 00 717832 8**, West Highland White Terrier **0 00 717831 X**,
Yorkshire Terrier **0 00 717606 6**

144pp £7.99

To order any of these titles please telephone **0870 787 1732**
For further information about Collins books visit our website:
www.collins.co.uk